Embrace the Face: Scars Show Strength – Tells YourStory, as You Walk in Purpose

© 2025 Duerre Thomas

All rights reserved.

No part of this book may be copied, reproduced, stored in a retrieval system, or transmitted in any form or by any means—electronic, mechanical, photocopying, recording, scanning, or otherwise—without prior written permission from the publisher, except for brief quotations in critical reviews or articles.

Published by:

Making A Difference Publishing

23456 Junction AVE

Port Charlotte, FL, 33980

ISBN:978-0-9857798-3-2

Unless otherwise indicated, all Scripture quotations are taken from the New International Version (NIV) of the Bible. Copyright © 1973,1978, 1984, 2011 by Biblica, Inc.™ Used by permission. All rights reserved worldwide.

Some names and identifying details have been changed to protect individuals' privacy.

For more information, visit:

Relevantflorida.com

Printed in the United States of America.

Endorsements

Few stories have the power to change the way you think and strengthen your faithlike this one. Duerre's journey is a powerful example of God's grace, and hiswords will not only inspire you but also give you the confidence to step into your purpose, no matter your limitations.

Sam Masteller, Senior Pastor, Freedom Life Church

I have known Duerre Thomas for 16 years and have been beside him in good times and in bad times. I have witnessed times of heartbreak that would be beyond most people's ability to endure. I have watched God shape and mold him to be a powerful voice for the Kingdom of God. His testimony is one I have heard many times, yet each time, I am profoundly moved by the undeniable hand of Almighty God on his life.

"Embrace the Face" is a powerful ,life-changing book and a testament to God's unfailing purpose for our lives. It reminds us that God does not make mistakes and no matter what the enemy has used to try and defeat us, we are more than conquerors through Him. Filled with wisdom, encouragement, and divine truth, this book will empower you to rise above adversity and walk boldly in the destiny God has designed for you. Don't let your struggles define you...God already has. A must-read for anyone whether you feel defeated or strong in your faith and who you are.

Kevin Gagnon, Portland ME,

"Embrace the Face is more than a book—it is a powerful manifesto for hope and healing. With wisdom and grace, Duerre reminds us that every scar carries a story worth telling. This inspiring work invites you to confront your deepest wounds and embrace the truth that God is not finished writing your story. Get ready to watch your life go to another level!"

TODD BISHOP

Lead Pastor - Church Unleashed

Author of Prosperity Unleashed, Leadership Unleashed, Leveraging Tension,& The Human Right

"Duerre takes readers on a powerful journey of learning to embrace every part of their story—scars and all—for the glory of God. I've had the privilege of walking in friendship with Duerre and have watched his testimony unfold in real time. His life is living proof that our scars carry power, purpose, and a message worth sharing.

Embrace the Face is a compelling reminder that God truly works all things together for our good. This book is a must-read for anyone who needs encouragement, healing, and the courage to embrace their testimony."

Endorsement – Pastor Dave Gargano

Founder & Lead Pastor, Road to Life Church, Indiana

Dedication

This book is dedicated to the ones who have shaped me, stood by me, and believed in the call of God on my life—even when I wrestled with my own doubts.

To my wife, Sharai – Your unwavering love, support, and faith have been a rock in my life. Thank you for standing by me in purpose all these years, for believing when I couldn't see, and for walking this journey with grace, strength, and relentless devotion.

To my four sons—D'Mari, Damir, Shamir, and Dashaun – My greatest hope is that you remember the example I lived out. May you emulate the faith I had—even greater. Embrace your scars, stand in confidence, and know that God can turn pain into purpose and scars into strength.

To the people of Relevant KingdomCenter – Thank you for trusting me to lead you, even with my limp. Your faith and dedication inspire me, and I pray this book encourages you to run boldly toward God's plans.

To my family – Especially my grandmothers, who poured into me, loved me, and stood by me. Your prayers and presence have been the foundation of my faith.

To the leaders and mentors who saw beyond my scars and pulled the purpose out of me—thank you for guiding me toward God's grace when I needed it most.

Finally, this book is for every person who has ever felt disqualified because of their scars.

God is about to turn your ashes into beauty, your pain into praise, and your wounds into weapons for His glory.

You were never disqualified—only destined.

Embrace your scars, and watch what God does next.

Foreword

You ever met someone and thought, **"Wow, this person has such an unbelievably powerful story to tell!"** That's exactly how we felt when we first met the unstoppable force that is **Duerre Thomas**—a man who carries himself with a **defiant, unshakable confidence** that declares, *"I've been through hell, but I refuse to be broken."*

And he's not just standing—**he's soaring!**

Embrace the Face is not just another Christian feel-good book. We think you'll find it **raw, unfiltered, and profoundly real**. It's packed with the kind of **hard-earned wisdom** that only comes from **personally walking through the fire—and emerging not just singed, but refined, fortified, and fearless!**

His story isn't merely about the **visible scars etched into his skin**. It's about his **deep, internal battles**. You know, the kind that **shake your soul, test your faith, and leave you staring at the heavens, whispering, "God—seriously? This is Your plan?" Because the truth is, **we all carry scars**. Some are carved into our flesh; others are **buried so deep that only our hearts know they exist**. *(Have you been there?)* That's precisely why this book is for you.

We love how Duerre never **sugar coats or sanitizes the truth**. He doesn't try to pretty up the pain and tie it with a neat little bow. **He tells it straight**. Yes, life **brutally and mercilessly knocked him down**—but God had a plan to **lift him higher than he ever imagined and** let's be honest, **God's plans? They rarely make sense to us at first**.

When we try to **stitch together our own broken pieces—we fail. Miserably.** But as you'll read in these pages, when we truly **surrender to God's purpose**, He takes those **shattered fragments** and forges something **infinitely stronger and breathtakingly beautiful!**

We gotta warn you—this isn't a **skim- through-it, nod-a-few-times kind of book**. This is a **sit-down, grab-a-highlighter, underline-like-crazy, have-a-few-"OMG"-moments** kind of book. If you're like us, you'll find yourself **laughing one moment, crying the next**, and then—out of nowhere—**feelingGod's voice thunder through your soul**.

So, get ready to be **challenged and transformed**. Get ready to see your own scars—however jagged, however painful—in a **whole new light.** Not as **evidence of suffering**, but as **undeniable proof of God's ultimate power, His love, and His relentless ability to redeem.**

Pastor Duerre, our dear friend, we are profoundly grateful that you **stepped up—despite the scars, the doubts, and the pain—and boldly said "yes" to God's calling.** We know that because of your **inspirational journey**, so many others will find the **courage to do the same.**

David and Nicole Crank
Lead Pastors of FaithChurch.com

Introduction

Scars tell stories.

They are proof that we've been through something—proof that we've faced battles, endured pain, and survived what should have taken us out. But too often, we hide our scars.

We cover them up, ashamed of what they reveal. We let them remind us of our pain rather than our survival.

For years, I struggled with my own visible scars—the ones on my face that told a story before I could even open my mouth.

• I wondered if people would ever see beyond them.

• I questioned if they would hold me back from my calling.

• I feared that they would always define me more than my words ever could.

But I have come to learn something life-changing— Scars don't disqualify you. They qualify you.

They are not a sign of weakness—they are a sign of resilience.

They are not a sign of defeat—they are a sign of God's grace.

The enemy wants to keep you ashamed of your scars because he knows they are the very thing that proves God's power at work in your life.

Why This Book?

Embrace the Face is not just about my story—it's about your story too.

• Maybe your scars aren't visible, but they're emotional, mental, or spiritual.

• Maybe life has left wounds on your heart that no one else can see.

• Maybe you've walked through seasons of shame, fear, or rejection, believing that your pain has disqualified you from purpose.

But here's what I want you to know: God is not ashamed of your scars.

He does not call you by your pain—He calls you by your purpose.

He does not see you through the lens of your past—He sees you through the lens of your destiny.

You were never meant to hide—you were meant to shine.

Matthew 5:14-16 reminds us:

"You are the light of the world. A city set on a hill cannot be hidden... let your light shine before others, that they may see your good deeds and glorify your Father in heaven."

It's time to stop hiding your story and start owning it. What You Will Discover

In these pages, we will journey together through the lessons I've learned about:

Overcoming insecurity and walking in godly confidence

Breaking free from shame and embracing who God created you to be

Understanding how your pain is connected to your purpose

Stepping boldly into your calling, knowing that your past does not disqualify you

Each chapter will challenge you to look at your scars differently, not as a source of shame but as a sign of strength

The Challenge

By the time you finish this book, I pray you will be able to:

- Look in the mirror and embrace the person God has created you to be.

- Stop apologizing for your story and start sharing it boldly.

- Recognize that your scars are not your weakness—they are your weapon.

- Step into your purpose with the confidence that you were made for more. Because the truth is:

You have survived for a reason.

Your story is not over.

And God is not done with you yet.

Now—let's begin the journey of embracing the face.

Contents

1. The Mirror Doesn't Lie, But It Doesn't Define You ... 1
2. Scarred but Still Standing ... 14
3. From Wounds to Warriors ... 24
4. Shame Off You - When shame becomes a shadow ... 37
5. When Pain Speaks, Purpose Answers ... 51
6. The Face of Grace - Embracing God's Work in You ... 64
7. Battle-Tested, Purpose-Approved ... 79
8. The Labels They Gave vs. The Name God Called ... 90
9. Made for More ... 97
10. Embrace the Face - Owning Your Story Without Fear ... 108
11. Bottom Line - Call to Action ... 117

REFLECTIONS ... 124

Acknowledgements ... 126

Final Author's Note ... 128

Additional Resources	132
Books by Duerre Thomas	134
Scripture Index	136
About the Author	143

Chapter 1

The Mirror Doesn't Lie, But It Doesn't Define You

We all have moments when we stare into the mirror and struggle to recognize the person looking back at us. The reflection may tell the truth about what is visible, but it doesn't always reveal the deeper reality of who we truly are. The mirror shows the surface—the scars, the imperfections, the features we wish we could change—but it cannot define the worth, purpose, or calling placed inside of us by God.

For years, I wrestled with this tension. I remember being a child, standing in front of the mirror, tracing my fingers over the scars on my face, wondering why I had to be the one who looked different. The world around me was quick to make judgments, offering stares, whispers, and at times, even cruel words. Society often tells us that our value is tied to appearance, but I had to learn that God's definition of me went far beyond what I could see in my reflection.

One of the greatest challenges we face in life is separating what we see from what we believe. Too often, we allow external realities to dictate internal truths. But here's the good news: What you see in the mirror is only part of your story—it's not the whole picture.

Redefining Identity Through God's Eye

The world may define you by your outward appearance, but God defines you by His purpose. The story of David is a powerful reminder of this truth. When the prophet Samuel went to anoint the next king of Israel, he looked at Jesse's sons and was drawn to those who had the outward stature of a king. But God reminded him:

> "The Lord does not look at the things people look at. People look at the outward appearance, but the Lord looks at the heart." — 1 Samuel 16:7 (NIV)

David was overlooked because he didn't fit the mold of what people expected a king to look like. But God saw something greater in him. Likewise, your worth is not measured by the world's standards but by the divine calling placed on your life.

In the same way, Jesus Himself did not fit the world's idea of what a king should look like. The Bible tells us in Isaiah 53:2 (NIV):

> "He had no beauty or majesty to attract us to him, nothing in his appearance that we should desire him."

Imagine that—the eternal King, the Son of God, did not have the appearance that people expected. He didn't look like royalty, and He didn't come in a way that demanded attention through outward stature. Yet, He was the King within—the Messiah sent to redeem the world.

Sometimes, people will overlook greatness because they are too focused on outward appearances. Sometimes, we even overlook ourselves because we focus on what we lack rather than who God has called us to be. Just as Jesus' worth and royalty were not defined by His outward appearance, our greatness and purpose are not dictated by what we look like or by others' opinions.

The Power of Words and Perception

Growing up, I experienced first hand the sting of words that reinforced my insecurities. There were moments when people's comments made me feel less than, unworthy, or even invisible. But I had to make a choice: Would I allow their words to shape my identity, or would I trust the truth of what God said about me?

Proverbs 18:21 reminds us:

"The tongue has the power of life and death."

We can choose to accept the labels placed upon us by others, or we can declare the identity God has given us. I had to learn to speak life over myself, to replace every negative word with

God's promises. If you've ever felt defined by someone else's words, know this—you have the power to break free from that narrative.

Turning Reflection into Revelation

Instead of allowing the mirror to dictate who you are, let it remind you of how far you've come. The scars you carry—whether physical or emotional—are not marks of shame; they are testimonies of survival. Every time I look in the mirror now, I don't see pain—I see purpose. I see evidence of God's grace, His healing, and His faithfulness.

Your reflection is not your definition. Your identity is not found in the world's approval, in the opinions of others, or in the wounds of your past. It is found in the One who created you with intentionality and purpose.

So today, I challenge you—stand in front of the mirror, but don't just see yourself through human eyes. See yourself as God sees you. Look beyond the scars, beyond the flaws, beyond the doubts, and embrace the truth: You are fearfully and wonderfully made (Psalm 139:14).

No more Filters

We live in a world obsessed with appearances. In our social media-driven culture, the need to impress people with our lives has become such a priority that we do so at the expense of being true to our reality. We go to extremes to make it seem like we are who we're not or that we have what we really don't—all to feel accepted by others.

In its truest sense, a filter is something that removes impurities or unwanted elements that might contaminate. But in the context of social media, a filter is a way to distort the facts and hide our flaws—something that makes us appear as something or someone we're not.

A lot of people get fooled by filters and end up being catfished and confused. They see a version of reality that doesn't truly exist. The danger is that this kind of filtered living doesn't just happen online—it becomes a mindset. We start living life hiding behind a mask, refusing to be real and authentic with ourselves and others.

The Reality of Filters

The truth is, we all use filters. The way we respond to our world around us is determined by the filter through which we see it. Filters are what produce emotions, and our feelings are filtered through our emotions.

Feelings are conscious, emotional experiences that contribute to thoughts, language, decision-making, and behavior. Emotions like anger, fear, joy, sadness, disgust, and surprise are shaped by the filters we carry.

The way we respond to circumstances, people, adversity, or even success is determined by the filters we use. Here's the thing most people don't realize—even the way we see ourselves is influenced and dictated by the filters we use.

Life and experiences put filters onus through which we view ourselves and our circumstances. And the filters we look through affect how we live.

• People who have been through betrayal will filter relationships differently from those who haven't.

• People who have experienced grief and loss will filter life differently from those who've never faced that kind of pain.

• People who have been through church hurt will filter church differently from those who haven't experienced it.

The problem arises when we start to filter our identity through the lens of pain and past experiences. We end up defining ourselves based on how we were treated, how we were wounded, or how we felt rejected.

Fixing the Flawed Filter

Fixing the not-so-lovely details is easy to do with an app, but it's a lot harder in this broken world—and even more difficult when it comes to fixing flaws within ourselves. That's why I value having honest people in my circle who aren't afraid to challenge me and help me grow.

I can't afford to get offended by everyone who doesn't always agree with me. We can't walk together unless we agree in purpose, direction, and mission—but we can walk together if you're willing to help me get better! Sometimes, getting better means addressing internal issues that may be constricting my growth.

There are things I know I need to fix, but there are also things I may not know because I'm blind to those areas that are broken. That's why it's so important to surround yourself with people who care enough to speak truth—not just those who will validate your filters.

The Filter of God's Word

Regardless of our life experiences, we must be willing to live life without the filter of this world's perspective so we can live life through the filter of God's Word and His perspective.

The filter of the Word helps to keep out the impurities that contaminate and confuse our lives. It shifts our view from self-centeredness to God-centeredness, reminding us that our identity is not shaped by opinions or circumstances but by God's truth.

1 Samuel 16:7 (NIV) says:

"But the Lord said to Samuel, 'Do not look on his appearance or on the height of his stature, because I have rejected him. For the Lord sees not as man sees: man looks on the outward appearance, but the Lord looks on the heart.'"

People were quick to dismiss David because he didn't look like a king. But God saw the heart and chose him for greatness. In the same way, we may feel overlooked or insignificant because we don't fit the world's standards, but God knows the potential and purpose within us.

God's perspective removes the filters of insecurity, fear, and rejection, allowing us to see ourselves as He sees us—loved, called and chosen.

Application: How to See Yourself Through God's Eyes

1. Speak Life Over Yourself

The power of words is undeniable. Proverbs 18:21 reminds us, **"The tongue has the power of life and death, and those who love it will eat its fruit."**

This means that the way we speak about ourselves can either build us up or tear us down. It's easy to repeat the negative words that others have spoken over us or the lies we've convinced ourselves are true. But God challenges us to align our speech with His truth.

Application: Start your day by declaring God's truth over your life:

- "I am fearfully and wonderfully made" (Psalm 139:14).
- "I am called and chosen by God" (1 Peter 2:9).
- "I am not defined by my past—I am shaped by God's purpose" (Jeremiah 29:11).

Challenge yourself to replace negative self-talk with declarations of truth.

Write down at least three affirmations rooted in Scripture and repeat them daily.

2. Stop Letting Appearances Define You

The world often emphasizes outward beauty, but God sees deeper. In 1 Samuel 16:7, the Lord said, **"The Lord does not look at the things people look at. People look at the outward appearance, but the Lord looks at the heart."**

David wasn't chosen because of his stature or looks but because of his heart.Similarly, God isn't impressed by outward perfection but by inward obedience and faithfulness.

Application: Reflect on an area where you've felt overlooked or undervalued because of your appearance or past. Pray and ask God to help you see yourself throughHis eyes. Write down what God says about you rather than what the world says.

3. See Your Scars as Signposts, Not Stop Signs

Your scars tell a story of survival and triumph. In 2 Corinthians 4:8-9, Paul declares,
"We are hard pressed on every side, but not crushed; perplexed, but not in despair; persecuted, but not abandoned; struck down, but not destroyed."
Your scars are not symbols of shame; they are markers of how God has kept you. Instead of trying to hide them, use them as a testimony of His grace and goodness.

Application: Write down one of your personal scars (physical or emotional) and how God has brought you through that situation. Pray for the courage to share that story with someone who needs to hear it.

4. Break Free from the Mirror's Lies

James 1:23-24 says,**"Anyone who listens to the word but does not do what it says is like someone who looks at his**

face in a mirror and, after looking at himself, goes away and immediately forgets what he looks like."

The mirror can show us our flaws, but it doesn't define who we are in Christ.Instead of allowing the mirror to speak lies, let God's Word be your mirror ,reflecting His love and acceptance.

Application: Stand in front of the mirror and declare these truths:

- **"God has not given me a spirit of fear, but of power, love, and a sound mind" (2 Timothy 1:7).**

- **"I am God's masterpiece, created in Christ Jesus to do good works" (Ephesian 2:10).**

- **"I am not a mistake—I am chosen and appointed to bear fruit" (John 15:16).**

Every time doubt creeps in, speak life over yourself and let God's Word affirm your identity.

Bottom Line: No Filter

Living filtered may look good on social media, but it will distort your reality and block your growth.

God doesn't want you to live behind a mask—He wants you to be real, raw, and redeemed.

Take off the filters and allow God to show you who you truly are.

Reflection Questions

When you look in the mirror, what thoughts immediately come to mind? Are they aligned with how God sees you?

What past wounds or insecurities have tried to define your identity?

How can you shift your perspective to see yourself through God's eyes?

What scriptural truths can you use to replace the negative filters in your life?

What practical steps can you take to stop seeing your scars as symbols of shame and start seeing them as signs of God's grace?

Scriptural References:

1. 1 Samuel 16:7 (NIV) - "The Lord does not look at the things people look at. People look at the outward appearance, but the Lord looks at the heart."

2. Isaiah 53:2 (NIV) - "He had no beauty or majesty to attract us to him, nothing in his appearance that we should desire him."

3. Proverbs 18:21 (NIV) - "The tongue has the power of life and death."

4. Psalm 139:14 (NIV) - "I praise you because I am fearfully and wonderfully made; your works are wonderful, I know that full well."

5. 1 Samuel 16:7 (NIV) - "The Lord sees not as man sees: man looks on the outward appearance, but the Lord looks on the heart."

Chapter 2
Scarred but Still Standing

Scars tell two stories—one of pain and one of perseverance. For years, I saw my scars as reminders of what I had been through, but I didn't recognize them as proof that I had survived. I only saw the struggle, not the strength. But God began to shift my perspective.

Life has a way of wounding us. Some wounds are physical, while others cut much deeper, into our emotions, our self-worth, and our faith. Maybe you've faced rejection, betrayal, loss, or personal failure. Maybe your scars are the result of something someone else did to you. Regardless of their origin, every scar carries weight, and the enemy would love for us to see them only as symbols of shame.

But here's the truth—scars are not signs of defeat; they are evidence of healing. The fact that you're still here, still standing, still pressing forward is proof that what was meant to destroy you did not succeed. The Bible reminds us in 2 Corinthians 4:8-9, "We are hard-pressed on every side, but not crushed; perplexed, but not in despair; persecuted, but not abandoned;

struck down, but not destroyed." I didn't realize it at the time, but even in my brokenness, God's grace was sustaining me.

Scars tell stories—stories of battles fought, pain endured, and victories won.

But too often, we hide them. We cover them up, ashamed of the past they reveal. In this chapter, I want to take you through a journey where scars became a symbol of survival rather than a sign of shame.

Growing up, I had to learn how to stand strong despite my scars—both physical and emotional. I had to face ridicule, rejection, and self-doubt head-on. But through it all, I discovered that God's grace and strength carried me through.

A Childhood Marked by Loss and Longing

My story didn't start with strength. It started with survival. I know what it means to carry scars that go beyond the surface. Losing both of my parents at a young age left an emotional void that, at times, felt impossible to fill. That kind of loss doesn't just wound—it reshapes you. It leaves questions that linger: Why me? Why did this happen? It's a grief that doesn't simply fade away but becomes a companion in life's journey.

My mother's life was one of resilience in the face of hardship. She endured abuse—something no woman should ever have to suffer. I witnessed her struggle, and though I was young, I felt the weight of her pain. I could feel the weight of her struggles.

Those moments left deep emotional scars, teaching me at an early age how cruel the world could be. They also planted seeds of resilience in me, though at the time, I didn't recognize them.

Yet even in the midst of this pain, God had a plan. Psalm 34:18 says, "The Lord is close to the brokenhearted and saves those who are crushed in spirit." Though I didn't always feel it, He was near, holding me up in moments when I thought I would collapse under the weight of my circumstances.

When Pain Takes a Physical Form

The emotional weight I carried soon began to manifest in a physical way. Lesions appeared on my face, each one feeling like a public announcement of my private pain. I could see the stares, hear the whispered conversations, and feel the quiet judgment. My face became a billboard of brokenness, and I couldn't escape it. I hated the mirror, hated what looked back at me—hated how every glance from others seemed to remind me that I was different.

The doctors in Nassau, Bahamas, thought it was ringworm at first and treated me accordingly. But the lesions spread and worsened, each new mark a fresh wound to my spirit.

The physical pain was bad enough, but the real torment was the shame and insecurity it birthed. Every new scar felt like a verdict: You're damaged, You're different. You'll never be normal.

My maternal grandmother did her best to take care of me, but I was sinking. As the scars grew, so did my frustration and anger. It wasn't just my face that felt disfigured—it was my spirit. I lashed out more, withdrew more, and the walls I built around my heart grew thicker. I didn't just feel ugly—I felt unseen, insignificant, and unworthy of love.

When the Darkness Feels Unbearable

There are moments when the pain doesn't just hurt—it consumes. It wraps itself around your heart like a vice, squeezing until you can't breathe. I was just a boy—barely old enough to understand life, let alone death—but I knew one thing: I couldn't take it anymore.

I still remember that day so vividly. The sun was shining outside, but it felt like shadows were pressing in on me from every side. I had spent the day avoiding mirrors and dodging people's glances. Every look felt like a silent judgment, like they could see straight through to my insecurities.

I didn't recognize myself anymore. My face—my very identity—felt like it had been stolen from me, replaced by a mask that broadcasted my brokenness to the world. It wasn't just the physical pain of the lesions—it was the suffocating shame that settled in my chest like a heavy stone. I felt ugly. Unwanted. Abandoned.

I couldn't see a way out. The thought that I'd never be normal, never be accepted, haunted me. It wasn't just the scars on my face—it was the scars on my soul, cut deeper by the whispers, the looks, and the feeling of being fundamentally flawed.

Despair became a companion. It whispered lies in the quiet, convincing me that my life was over before it had even begun. I didn't want to face another day—another glance that reminded me of how disfigured I looked. I didn't want to live with the constant ache of being different. I wanted to disappear, to escape the pain that clung to me like a relentless shadow.

So I decided I was done fighting. I wrapped myself in a blanket, crept into the closet, and found a can of gasoline. I wasn't thinking logically—I just wanted the pain to stop. As I poured the gas around me and struck the match, my hands were shaking—not from fear, but from the overwhelming grief of a child who felt completely lost.

As the flame caught, I curled into a ball, pulling the blanket tighter around me. The smell of gasoline filled the air, mixing with the bitter scent of hopelessness. Tears streamed down my face, hot and unchecked. I squeezed my eyes shut, bracing myself for the end.

But then—bang. A loud, urgent knock. It startled me out of my spiral. My uncle's voice called out from the other side of the door, offering lunch—Kraft dinner and cheese, my favorite. The smell of smoke was already creeping under the door, and he didn't wait for a response. He barged in, eyes widening at the sight of the flames. He didn't yell, didn't reprimand me—he just put out the fire and pulled me into his arms.

I couldn't hold it in anymore. I broke down in sobs, clutching his shirt, afraid to look him in the eyes. I was ashamed—ashamed that I wanted to die, ashamed that I couldn't handle the weight of my own reflection. He didn't lecture me or scold me. He just held me, whispering that I was going to be okay. For the first time in what felt like forever, I believed him.

Finding Hope in the Ashes

Looking back, I realize that God sent my uncle at that exact moment to save me from myself. It wasn't just about stopping the fire—it was about reminding me that I wasn't alone. The enemy wanted me to believe that my story was over, that my life was a waste. But God knew better. God knew that one day I would stand on platforms, scars and all, proclaiming His goodness.

In that moment of despair, I didn't have the strength to call on God. But He didn't wait for me to reach out—He intervened before I could make a mistake that would have ended everything. It was grace that knocked on my door that day. It was love that refused to let me go.

Psalm 34:18 says,

> "The Lord is close to the brokenhearted and saves those who are crushed in spirit."

That day, I was crushed—more than I had ever been before. But God met me there. He saw past my brokenness and knew that my pain had a purpose. He saw the preacher I would become, the husband I would be, and the lives that would be impacted by my testimony.

My story wasn't over. In fact, it was just beginning.

Standing Because He Keeps Us

This story serves as a reminder that we're still standing because God is a keeper. No matter the wounds, no matter the scars—we're still here.

When I think about how God has preserved me from death, from pain, from loss, and even from myself, I know it wasn't by my strength or my ability to protect myself—it was God.

He's kept me for a purpose.

He's guarded me for a reason.

And as long as He keeps me standing, I know He still has my life covered by his hand

Decision that shaped my Destiny

In response to my growing struggles, my family made a decision that would mark a major turning point in my life—I was sent to Freeport, Bahamas, to live with my paternal grandparents. At the time, I didn't fully understand what was happening, but looking back, I see how God was moving. What felt like another loss, another rejection, was actually the first major shift in my destiny.

Romans 8:28 reminds us that,

"in all things God works for the good of those who love him, who have been called according to his purpose." What seemed like abandonment was really preparation for something greater.

Bottom Line:

Your scars are not symbols of shame; they are reminders that you survived. What was meant to break you only became proof of God's grace at work in your life.

Reflection Questions

What scars (physical or emotional) have shaped your journey? Are you still allowing them to define you?

How has God shown you His grace in the areas where you felt broken or unworthy?

What lessons have you learned from the pain you've endured? How have they made you stronger?

Who in your life needs to hear your story of overcoming? How can you share it with them?

What steps can you take to stop seeing your scars as weaknesses and start seeing them as evidence of survival?

Scripture References & Citations

1. 2 Corinthians 4:8-9 - "We are hard-pressed on every side, but not crushed..."

2. Psalm 34:18 - "The Lord is close to the brokenhearted and saves those who are crushed in spirit."

3. Isaiah 61:3 - "Beauty for ashes, the oil of joy for mourning..."

(All scriptural references are cited from the Holy Bible, New International Version (NIV) and King James Version (KJV).)

Chapter 3
From Wounds to Warriors

Moving to Freeport was more than just a geographical shift—it was a defining moment in my life. I was stepping into a new environment, one that would challenge me, shape me, and ultimately prepare me for my calling. But at the time, all I could feel was uncertainty.

Freeport was different. The culture, the people, the way of life—it all felt unfamiliar. I had to adjust quickly, learning how to navigate a new household with my paternal grandparents. They were loving and firm, determined to instill values in me that would help me stand strong despite my struggles. But even with their love, I wrestled with feelings of abandonment, rejection, and anger.

Faith, Structure, and Discipline

My grandmother was a devout believer. Going to church wasn't optional—it was required. Every Sunday, we would walk up the road to Calvary Temple Assemblies of God, where my grandmother worshiped with unshakable faith. She was the one who introduced me to the power of prayer, and though I didn't fully grasp it at the time, she was planting seeds of faith that would later sustain me.

Proverbs 22:6 says,

"Train up a child in the way he should go, and when he is old he will not depart from it." Looking back, I can see how her discipline in faith was shaping my foundation.

In our home, there was structure. My grandfather, a man of discipline, believed in hard work, respect, and integrity. He taught me the value of responsibility, of taking pride in what I did, even in the small things. At the time, I didn't appreciate it as much as I should have, but now I see how God used those lessons to mold me into the man I would become.

A Devastating Diagnosis

Despite the structure and stability, my grandmother sensed there was more to my condition than what the doctors in Nassau had suggested. With unwavering determination, she decided to take me to a private doctor in Freeport. I was 12 years old at the time, completely unaware that this visit would change my life forever.

After a series of tests and examinations, the doctor delivered a devastating diagnosis: Discoid Lupus. And with it came a prognosis that shattered me even further—because the disease was active, they didn't see me living past 18 years old.

At that moment, the weight of those words crushed both my grandmother and me. I saw the sorrow in her eyes, the silent prayers she whispered under her breath. As for me, I felt like I was drowning in despair. Tears streamed down my face as I sat on the edge of the examination table, grappling with a reality I never saw coming. My mind raced back to the painful nights I watched my mother endure, how Lupus had slowly taken a toll on her body, eventually claiming her life.

And now, here I was, sitting in a doctor's office, staring at my own mortality.

I remember looking up, tears falling freely, and asking God, "WHY ME?" The pain, the fear, the confusion—it all came rushing in. I felt abandoned by life, by fate, and for a moment, even by God. But I wasn't alone.

Psalm 61:2 says,

> "From the end of the earth I will cry to You, when my heart is overwhelmed; lead me to the rock that is higher than I."

Though I couldn't see it in that moment, God was still writing my story. This diagnosis wasn't my ending—it was the beginning of something greater.

A Church That Covered Me

News of my diagnosis spread through my church community. By this time, I had started becoming more involved at Calvary Temple Assemblies of God. Friday nights, I attended CA's (Christ Ambassadors) youth meetings. Sunday mornings, I was committed to Sunday School. Wednesdays, I became part of a boys' club calledRoyal Rangers, which taught discipline, leadership, and biblical principles.

The church wasn't just a place I went—it was becoming a part of who I was.

Because of my grandmother's unwavering commitment to keeping me in the presence of God,I had already been exposed to the reality of heaven and hell. I knew there was life after this one, and that eternity was real.

In that moment of despair, I made the most important decision of my life—I gave my heart to Jesus. I wasn't sure what the future held, but I knew one thing: If I was going to die, I wasn't going to hell!

Romans10:9 says,

> "If you declare with your mouth, 'Jesus is Lord,' and believe in your heart that God raised him from the dead, you will be saved."

That day, I believed, and my life would never be the same.

A Divine Encounter in My Room

One afternoon, as I sat alone in my room, something stirred in my spirit. I felt led to do something out of the ordinary—to take my Bible, open it randomly, and read the first scripture my eyes landed on.

It was an act of desperation, a silent cry for hope.

As I flipped open the pages, my eyes fell on Psalm 118:17:

> "I will not die but live, and will proclaim what the Lord has done."

At that moment, something inside of me shifted. It was as if God Himself had reached down and spoken directly to me. I held onto that scripture like a lifeline.

Though the doctors had spoken death over me, God had spoken life.

Isaiah 55:11 says,

> "So is my word that goes out from my mouth: It will not return to me empty, but will accomplish what I desire and achieve the purpose for which I sent it."

God's word was greater than any medical prognosis, and I chose to believe it.

A Life-Changing Experience: My MarchingOrders

Not long after this, my church decided to do something special for me. At 13 years old, they sponsored me to attend Summer Youth Camp in Abaco during Teen Week, covering all expenses.

WhatI didn't know was that this trip would be an encounter with God that would confirm everything He had spoken to me in the isolation of my room.

During one of our chapel nights, we had a guest speaker from Chicago named Titus Lee. He had a powerful prophetic ministry, and as he ministered, he suddenly called me out.

"Young man, I don't know your story, but God said to tell you... if you preach for Him, you will live and not die!"

I was blown away.

Only weeks before, in the privacy of my room, God had spoken the very same words tome. There was no way Titus Lee could have known that. It was undeniable confirmation.

That night, something inside of me completely surrendered.

Right there at that altar, I made a covenant with God:

❖ As long as I live, I will preach.

❖ I will use my life as a testimony of His grace and goodness.

❖ I will declare His power and providence.

I had received my marching orders.

When Pain Becomes Purpose

The diagnosis of lupus didn't just challenge my body—it shook my identity. I was young, unprepared, and unsure of what the future held. I found myself questioning everything—my purpose, my potential, even my worth. It wasn't just a battle with my health; it was a battle with myself. I felt trapped in a body that seemed to betray me, and the weight of that reality threatened to crush my spirit.

But looking back now, I can see how that struggle shaped my resolve. It wasn't just about surviving the diagnosis; it was about learning to live with purpose despite it. I had to make a choice—to either allow the pain to paralyze me or to let it propel me into purpose.

God was teaching me something profound: My strength wasn't in my perfection or my physical wellness, but in my willingness to stand despite my wounds. It was in those moments of weakness that I found an inner resolve to rise, to fight, and to refuse to let sickness define me. That determination became a foundational part of my journey—not just as a person but as a leader.

Shaping Ministry from Pain

That resolve didn't just stay with me personally—it began to shape how I approached ministry. I couldn't just preach about overcoming without understanding the weight of the fight. I couldn't tell others to keep going if I hadn't faced the temptation to give up myself.

Every time I stepped onto a platform or sat across from someone sharing their own pain, I carried that awareness with me—the awareness that pain doesn't disqualify you from purpose. In fact, it deepens it. It gives you a voice that resonates with the broken because you've been broken too. It gives you compassion for the struggling because you've struggled too.

My determination to push through lupus became the fuel that ignited my passion for ministry. I knew that if God could strengthen me to stand through that, He could do the same for others. My scars became stories, and my wounds became weapons against the enemy's lies. Instead of letting pain silence me, I allowed it to speak through me.

I realized that God wasn't just allowing me to endure—He was equipping me. He was refining me, shaping me into a warrior who wouldn't just survive the battle but thrive through it. I was being prepared not just to preach about victory but to live it—even when it hurt.

Applying These Lessons to Your Own Story

Everyone of us will face moments in life where we feel abandoned, broken, or without hope. Maybe you weren't diagnosed with a terminal disease, but you've been given news that shook your world. Perhaps you've felt rejected, unseen, or like the odds are stacked against you. But just like God was working in my story, He is working in yours.

Here are some key takeaways from this chapter and how you can apply them to your own journey:

1. **Embrace Your Foundations**

Even when I didn't understand it, my grandmother made sure I was in church. She ensured that faith was being instilled in me, even when I was too young to fully grasp its power. Maybe you had someone in your life planting seeds of faith—or maybe you're the first in your family to break cycles of dysfunction.E ither way, God uses the foundation we build in faith to sustain us when the storms come.

Application: If you were raised in faith, take a moment to thank God for the people who poured into you. If you're just starting your faith journey, begin to surround yourself with people who will help you grow spiritually. Faith is the anchor that holds you when life shakes you.

2. Don't Let a Diagnosis Define You

The doctors said I wouldn't live past 18. But God had a different plan. Whether you've received bad news from a doctor, a teacher, a boss, or a family member, remember this: Their words do not have the final say over your life—God's Word does.

Application: What negative labels or limitations have been spoken over you? Write them down—and then replace them with what God says about you. Meditate on scriptures like Psalm 118:17 ("I will not die but live, and will proclaim what the Lord has done.") and declare them over your life daily.

3. Seek God in Your Desperation

The moment I cried out to God in my room and opened the Bible to Psalm 118:17 was a turning point for me. God met me in my desperation, and His Word became my foundation.

Application: If you are in a season of struggle, take time to seek God intentionally. Open His Word, spend time in prayer, and ask Him to speak to you. He is still speaking. You may be one moment away from hearing exactly what you need.

4. Believe in Divine Confirmation

God didn't just speak to me once—He confirmed it through a prophetic word from Titus Lee at youth camp. God is a God of confirmation. If He has spoken something to you, He will send the right people, the right circumstances, and the right moments to affirm what He has already placed in your heart.

Application: Pay attention to divine confirmations. Has God spoken something to you, but you're doubting it? Ask Him for confirmation. He will find a way to remind you of His promise.

5. Make a Covenant with God

That night at the altar, I made a commitment—I would preach as long as I lived. That commitment became a covenant. What God calls you to, He will sustain you through.

Application: What is God calling you to do? Have you fully surrendered your life to His plan? Take a moment to pray and make a commitment. It doesn't have to be preaching—but whatever He's leading you todo, say YES

Bottom Line:

God doesn't just want you to survive your struggle—He wants you to thrive through it. Your wounds are not a sign of defeat but a declaration that you are still standing, still fighting, and still called for purpose.

Reflection Questions

What battles have you fought that made you feel wounded or defeated? How did you find the strength to keep going?

Reflect on a time when God turned your wounds into a testimony. How did that impact your life and those around you?

What does it mean to you to become a warrior despite your wounds? How can you walk more confidently in that truth?

Who has been a warrior in your life, helping you overcome challenges? Have you thanked them for their support?

How can you use your story to encourage someone who feels too broken to keep fighting?

Scripture References & Citations

Proverbs 22:6 - "Train up a child in the way he should go, and when he is old he will not depart from it."

Psalm 61:2 - "From the end of the earth I will cry to You, when my heart is overwhelmed; lead me to the rock that is higher than I."

Romans 10:9 - "If you declare with your mouth, 'Jesus is Lord,' and believe in your heart that God raised him from the dead, you will be saved."

Psalm 118:17 - "I will not die but live, and will proclaim what the Lord has done."

Isaiah 55:11 - "So is my word that goes out from my mouth: It will not return to me empty, but will accomplish what I desire and achieve the purpose for which I sent it."

Chapter 4

Shame Off You - When shame becomes a shadow

Shame has a way of creeping in and settling into your spirit, like a shadow that follows you no matter how fast you try to run. I know what it's like to wear shame like a second skin—to feel like your past mistakes or your visible flaws define your worth.

There were moments when I couldn't escape the thoughts of inadequacy. Times when I felt like I wasn't enough—like my scars and my story made me less deserving of grace. It's a suffocating feeling, being trapped by your own insecurities. I remember moments when I would put on my best face, hoping that people wouldn't see the cracks underneath. I wanted to be bold, but deep down, I felt like a fraud—like I was trying to convince myself more than anyone else that I was confident.

I tried to ignore the pain, to mask it with ministry and performance. But shame doesn't just fade because you're busy—it lingers, whispering that you'll never be enough, never be loved, never be worthy. I felt like I was fighting a battleI couldn't win.

No matter how much I preached to others about freedom, I couldn't seem to get free myself.

Walking in Godly Confidence

There came a point where I realized I couldn't keep carrying that weight. It wasn't just slowing me down—it was suffocating my spirit. One day, in a moment of prayer, I broke down and laid it all before God. I didn't have the strength to hold it together anymore. I was tired of fighting for acceptance when I already had it through Christ.

That was the turning point. I had to confront the lie that my worth was determined by people's opinions or my own perfection. I had to face the reality that I was trying to prove myself when God never asked me to.

It hit me: I had been carrying shame that Jesus already paid for. Why was I letting something that was nailed to the cross keep haunting me?

Shame is a liar. It tells you that you are unworthy. It convinces you that you arenot enough. It holds you hostage to the past.

But here's the truth: God never intended for us to live in shame.

Romans8:1 declares,

"There is therefore now no condemnation for those who are in Christ Jesus."

Yet, many of us still struggle to walk freely because shame has convinced us that we are unqualified, unwanted, and unlovable.

Wearing the Mask

Growing up, I learned how to mask my insecurities well. Though my face bore the marks of my condition, I did everything I could to pretend it didn't bother me. I joked before others could. I made light of my scars before anyone had a chance to comment.

But deep down, I was hurting.

I walked into rooms with my head high, trying to convince myself that my scars didn't bother me, but deep down, I wondered if people were looking at me with curiosity, pity, or disgust.

How many times do we let the opinions of others define us? How many times do we wear a mask, pretending we are fine when inside, we are battling shame, insecurity, and self-doubt?

Maybe you weren't scarred physically like I was. But maybe you've been scarred emotionally, relationally, or spiritually. Maybe you've been rejected, ridiculed, or made to feel like you weren't enough. And now, you carry the shame of not being what others expected you to be.

One of the biggest lies shame tells us is that if people see the real us, they won't accept us. That we must cover up, shrink ourselves, or change to fit in.

But let me tell you—God never called us to fit in.

"I praise You because I am fearfully and wonderfully made; Your works are wonderful, I know that full well." - Psalm 139:14 (NIV)

WhenI finally realized this truth, I began to unlearn the lies and remove the mask.But that wasn't an easy journey.

But let me tell you what I've learned—God never intended for you to live in shame.

Isaiah61:7 says,

"Instead of your shame you will receive a double portion, and instead of disgrace you will rejoice in your inheritance. And so you will inherit a double portion in your land, and everlasting joy will be yours."

God replaces shame with joy. He exchanges our disgrace for His grace.

The Battle of My Teenage Years

Even after God touched my life, I was still not exempt from the normal experiences that teenagers go through. I didn't necessarily have it easy.

I was teased and taunted because of the lesions on my face and scalp. Kids would shun me at times, treating me as if my condition made me unworthy of their friendship. However, one of the most painful experiences I endured came not from kids—but from a teacher.

She didn't understand what the scars on my face were, and rather than asking, she assumed the worst. It was like she feared I would spread a disease in her class room.

Because of this, my learning was hindered. One day, she took it a step further. She called my paternal grandmother and my uncle into a conference to discuss what she saw as my "inability" to do well in her class. But instead of simply expressing concern, she spoke words that nearly crushed me.

"He is not fit to be in my classroom with 'normal' kids," she said coldly. "He belongs in a special school for mentally challenged children."

In one sentence, she labeled me.

In one sentence, she tried to define my future.

In one sentence, she tried to convince me that I was less than what God created me to be.

I felt the weight of her words pressing on me like a heavy blanket of shame. Was I really not smart enough? Was I really not good enough?

But here's the thing—she was wrong.

I continued to push through. I refused to let that shame dictate my future. By the time I reached the 10th grade, I had two homeroom teachers, Mrs. White and Mrs. Russell, who saw me for who I really was. They embraced me, encouraged me, and as a result of a healthier environment, I began to thrive.

The more I was surrounded by acceptance instead of rejection, I started to believe in myself. My confidence grew, and I excelled in my later years of high school. Eventually, I graduated with honors.

But here's the part that still amazes me: years later, I was invited back to that same school as a keynote speaker.

And guess who was still teaching there?

That same teacher who once told my family that I didn't belong in a normal classroom.

The very student she thought would fail was now standing in front of an auditorium, speaking to hundreds, sharing my story of perseverance, faith, and confidence in God's plans.

God's Plans Are Greater

That experience almost tied me down in shame.

It nearly convinced me that I wasn't capable of success.

One thing I've learned is that God doesn't allow pain without a purpose.

I may not have understood it at the time, but everything I went through was preparing me for what was ahead.

There was a scripture that I held onto as time went on—Jeremiah 29:11:

"ForI know the plans I have for you," declares the Lord, "plans to prosper you and not to harm you, plans to give you hope and a future."

Shame tried to tell me I had no future, but God had already written one for me.

Shame told me I was a mistake, but God reminded me I was a masterpiece.

I had already endured rejection, whispers, and sideways glances—the world had made it clear that I was different. And different didn't always feel desirable.

When I was younger, I used to pray for my scars to disappear. I thought if God really loved me, He would wipe them away and make me look like everyone else. But instead of removing them, He left them—and He changed the way I saw them.

Because the truth is: God doesn't remove everything that makes us uncomfortable.Sometimes, He leaves it as a testament to His grace, His power, and His purpose.

But back then, I hadn't fully understood that yet. I still struggled with acceptance—not just self-acceptance, but the question that lingered in the back of my mind:

Would someone ever love me beyond my scars. the quiet prayers where I begged God to make me look like everyone else—I didn't realize that God was saying, "I didn't create you to blend in. I created you to stand out."

The Words That Stuck with Me

Before I left Freeport to attend college in Columbus, Ohio, Uncle Lynden made a joke that stuck with me more than I expected.

"If you ever find a woman who will kiss the scars on your face, that's how you'll know she is the one."

At the time, I laughed it off. It seemed impossible. The scars were there. They were obvious. They were a part of me that most people avoided looking at directly—much less embracing.

But God has a way of confirming things in the most unexpected ways.

The Silver Volvo Moment

By the time I met Sharai, I had mustered the confidence to ask her on a date. But even though I had grown in my self-assurance, there was still that small, quite question inside me.

Would she see beyond my scars?

We spent time getting to know one another, and the more I learned about her, the more I realized she wasn't like anyone else I had met.

Then came the moment that changed everything.

We were sitting in her silver Volvo, parked in a quiet spot, just talking. And then—without hesitation, without warning, without any sense of discomfort—she leaned over and kissed my face.

For a second, time froze.

All I could hear in my mind were the words Uncle Lynden had spoken before I left for college:

"If you ever find a woman who will kiss the scars on your face, that's how you'll know she is the one."

At that moment, I knew—this was the one God had for me.

She wasn't just loving a man—she was embracing my story, my past, my battles, and my future.

She was drawn to my essence, my heart, my purpose.

That moment in the silver Volvo wasn't just affection—it was affirmation.

It wasn't just a woman who liked me—this was a woman who embraced me, fully, without reservation.

And that moment reminded me of Genesis 24, where Rebekah's willingness to serve was a sign that she was meant to be Isaac's wife. The confirmation wasn't in a grand display—it was in a simple, pure act of love that spoke volumes.

> "Let the young woman to whom I shall say, 'Please let down your jar that I may drink,' and who shall say, 'Drink, and I will water your camels'—let her be the one whom you have appointed for your servant Isaac" (Genesis 24:14, ESV).

Just like Rebekah's response was a divine confirmation for Isaac, Sharai's kiss was confirmation for me.

From Shame to Strength

Shame clings to your past, but God calls you into your future.

Shame reminds you of your failures, but God redefines you with His favor.

Shame says you are disqualified, but God says you are destined.

I want you to hear this loud and clear: Shame is not your portion!

It's time to take shame off you and step into the confidence that God has already given you.

Shame will try to convince you that you're still chained to your past. But grace doesn't just set you free—it calls you to live like you're free. It's one thing to be declared forgiven, but it's another to walk in that freedom.

One of the most powerful lessons I've learned is that shame loses its grip when you expose it to the truth. It thrives in secrecy and isolation, but when you bring it to the light, it can't survive. I had to stop hiding and start speaking the truth over my life. I had to confront the lies with God's Word and remind myself that I am not defined by my past—I am defined by His grace.

That's why it's important to not just hear about freedom, but to live it out daily. You can't just quote Scripture—you have to apply it. You have to remind yourself that no weapon formed against you will prosper (Isaiah 54:17) and that nothing can separate you from God's love (Romans 8:38-39).

When shame tries to creep back in, confront it with truth. Speak over yourself that you are chosen, loved, and worthy. Declare that your identity is rooted in Christ, not in your past mistakes or external flaws.

How to start walking in godly confidence today:

1. See Yourself How God Sees You

The world will try to label you, but God has already named you.

Application: What negative labels have you placed on yourself? Write them down, then cross them out. Next to each one, write what God says about you. (Example: Instead of "Not enough" → Write "More than a conqueror" - Romans 8:37.)

2. Stop Apologizing for Who You Are

God didn't make a mistake when He created you. He wasn't distracted when He designed you.

Application: Make a declaration over yourself daily. Say out loud: "I am fearfully and wonderfully made. I am called and chosen. My past does not define me—God does!"

3. Walk in Your Purpose Boldly

Confidence comes from knowing you have a purpose. Shame tries to keep you from stepping into it.

Application: What's one thing God has placed on your heart that shame has held you back from pursuing? Take one bold step today toward it. Maybe it's starting the business, writing the book, speaking your testimony—do it afraid, but do it!

Bottom Line: Shame Off You

Shame has no place in the life of a child of God. You've been set free—so live like it. Break the silence, confront the lie, and walk boldly in the identity Christ has given you.

Reflection Questions

What shame have you been carrying that you need to let go of? How has it held you back?

Why is it important to separate your past mistakes from your identity? How can you make that shift today?

How does walking in Godly confidence look different from living in pride? Why is that distinction important?

What truth from Scripture can you hold on to when shame tries to creep back in?

How can you practically encourage someone else to walk in confidence despite their past?

Scripture References & Citations

Romans 8:1. There is therefore now no condemnation to them which are in Christ Jesus, who walk not after the flesh, but after the Spirit.

Isaiah 61:7 For your shame ye shall have double; and for confusion they shall rejoice in their portion: therefore in their land they shall possess the double: everlasting joy shall be unto them.

John 8:36 If the Son therefore shall make you free, ye shall be free indeed.

Psalm 139:14 I will praise thee; for I am fearfully and wonderfully made: marvelous are thy works; and that my soul knows right well.

Jeremiah 29:11 For I know the thoughts that I think toward you, saith the Lord, thoughts of peace, and not of evil, to give you an expected end.

Chapter 5
When Pain Speaks, Purpose Answers

Pain has a voice. It speaks loudly in the moments when life feels unfair, when the weight of struggle presses on your shoulders, and when the wounds of the past refuse to fade.

I know this because pain spoke to me.

It spoke in the loneliness of losing my parents.

It echoed in the taunts of classmates who didn't understand my scars.

It shouted in the voice of a teacher who told me I wasn't good enough.

It whispered in the late nights when I asked God, "Why me?"

And then, it screamed in ministry.

Pain doesn't just speak to you—it speaks for you. It tells a story. It shapes perspective. It builds resilience.

And for those who surrender their pain to God, pain becomes the platform where purpose is revealed.

Romans 8:28 reminds us,

> "And we know that in all things God works for the good of those who love Him, who have been called according to His purpose."

Marriage & Ministry: The Highs and Lows

I eventually got married and became the full-time Youth Pastor at Calvary Temple in Freeport. My wife, Sharai, and I were thriving. Our youth group grew from 12 to 180, and we built one of the largest youth conferences in the Bahamas, second only to Youth Alive.

We pushed boundaries, used untraditional ministry methods, launched TV and radio programs, and impacted the island in a major way. I traveled, spoke at churches on different islands, and later became the National Youth Director of The Assemblies of God.

Then came a moment that changed everything.

I was asked to move over to Exuma, Bahamas, to pastor a small church plant calledClear Water Assembly of God. Leaving Freeport wasn't easy. We had just built anew home. My grandmother was still alive. My Aunt Karen an uncle, Lynden, who had mentored me, was there. Everything in Freeport felt safe.

But God was calling us to step out in faith.

After visiting Exuma a few times, Sharai and I felt the nudge. We took a bold leap, packed up our four boys, and moved. We had no idea that while this move would bring incredible growth and impact, it would also bring some of our deepest wounds in ministry.

A Season of Growth and Resistance

Exuma was hungry for something different. I brought an unconventional style of ministry that attracted young people and families. Our church grew quickly. We launched LIVE GOD LOUD, a powerful outreach movement, feeding the hungry, helping single mothers with gas and groceries, and visiting the elderly living in poor conditions.

The church exploded with growth, but not everyone was happy.

The executive leadership of The Organization I was apart of—including my former pastor—began to push back. They didn't expect this much success. I approached them for expansion plans, but instead of excitement, I was met with resistance.

Kevin and Karla Gagnon, the missionary couple who had started the church, had donated large sums of money toward the ministry, but when we inquired about where those funds had gone, we were told not to ask.

I was crushed.

I had left everything in Freeport, believing this was God's move. But now I felt stuck. I was passionate, but I was powerless.

Then came the meeting that shook me.

The Superintendent and my former pastor flew in. They sat me down and told me that moving forward:

I was no longer the Lead Pastor.

I was to act as a manager, taking orders from them.

I was not to ask about finances.

I felt betrayed, belittled, and blindsided.

Pain was speaking again.

A Defining Decision: Birth of RKC

During this time, Kevin and Karla invited us to Maine, where we were embraced by their family and Pastor Dan Abatellio, the Superintendent of the Assemblies of God in Maine.

It was a place of healing.

It was there that Sharai and I heard God clearly—we needed to go back to Exuma, but this time, independently.

We made another bold leap of faith and planted Relevant Kingdom Center (RKC), a church for the de-churched and unchurched.

This time, we built on faith alone.

RKC became one of the fastest-growing churches on the island. We started a Sunday morning radio program called Power for Life. We launched outreach programs like "Pull Up for a Full Up", helping single mothers and the elderly with gas and food. Young professionals started attending. Lives were changing.

But the pain wasn't over yet.

Betrayals in Leadership

Leadership comes with highs and lows, but nothing prepared me for the devastation of betrayal—especially from someone I considered a brother. He wasn't just a leader on my team; he was a friend, someone I trusted with the vision God had given me. I had poured into him—my time, my energy, my prayers—believing he was called to stand alongside me in ministry. But betrayal doesn't come from enemies. It comes from those you least expect.

The revelation hit like a gut punch—embezzlement, mismanagement of resources, deceit. When the truth surfaced, I couldn't believe it. I kept thinking, Not him. Anyone but him. I didn't just feel betrayed by him—I felt betrayed by my own discernment. How did I miss the signs? How did I not see what was happening right under my nose?

Anger rose within me—hot, uncontrollable anger that made me want to call him out, confront him, demand answers. But right on its heels came confusion—doubt gnawing at my soul. Had I been too trusting? Was I too naive? Was I so focused on building the vision that I missed the cracks forming within the foundation?

That night, I sat alone in my office, fists clenched and heart racing. I felt like a fool. A leader who couldn't even see the deception brewing within his own camp. I questioned my own judgment. How could I stand in front of people, preach about integrity, and not see betrayal brewing behind me?

When Faith Feels Fragile

I couldn't shake the feeling that I had failed—failed the church, failed my family, failed God. The anger morphed into bitterness, and bitterness threatened to choke out my calling. I thought about quitting—leaving it all behind and walking away from ministry altogether. What was the point of pouring into people if they would just turn around and stab me in the back?

My prayers became desperate cries:

"God, why didn't You warn me? Why didn't You protect me from this? Why did You let me trust him?

I felt my faith waver. My confidence as a leader was fractured. It wasn't just about the betrayal anymore—it was about feeling like I didn't have what it took to lead. The very thing I feared most—being seen as inadequate—was staring me in the face.

I sat in silence, wrestling with the weight of the wound. I didn't want to forgive. I wanted justice, vindication—some kind of assurance that this wouldn't happen again. Yet in the stillness, God whispered something that stung even more than the betrayal:

"Forgive him."

How could I? How do you forgive someone who knew your heart, knew your vision, and still chose to betray you? I wasn't ready to let go of the hurt. I wasn't ready to release him from the blame.

But God didn't ask me to feel like forgiving—He just asked me to obey.

A Time to Heal

I knew I had a choice: stay bitter or let God heal the wound. I couldn't let the betrayal define me. I couldn't let one person's actions dismantle everything God had called me to build. So I did the hardest thing I've ever had to do—I forgave him. Not because I wanted to, but because I had to. My purpose was too great to let bitterness poison it.

It wasn't a one-time prayer. It was daily surrender—choosing to release the hurt every time it resurfaced. It meant admitting that I didn't have all the answers and trusting God to restore what betrayal tried to break. It meant asking God to heal not just the ministry but my heart.

Genesis 50:20 (NIV) says,

"You intended to harm me, but God intended it for good to accomplish what is now being done, the saving of many lives."

In my pain, I couldn't see how God could possibly use this for good. But as time went on, I began to understand that the betrayal didn't disqualify me—it refined me. It taught me to trust God's discernment more than my own and reminded me that no leader is above being hurt.

Rebuilding Trust and Confidence

When I finally allowed God to touch the wounded areas of my heart, He began to show me that forgiveness wasn't just about releasing the other person—it was about freeing myself. Holding onto bitterness kept me bound to the past. Letting go gave me permission to move forward.

Slowly, my confidence returned. I stopped questioning my calling and started asking God for wisdom to guard my heart while still being open to loving and leading people. I learned that betrayal doesn't define a leader—how they respond to it does.

God didn't just restore my confidence—He increased it. He showed me that despite being blindsided, I was still His chosen vessel. Despite being hurt, I was still called to lead. Despite being betrayed, I still had a purpose.

God Always Has a Plan

Just when I thought the betrayal would break the momentum of the ministry, God showed me that He always has a plan. In the middle of my pain, He reminded me that He is still the orchestrator of every detail.

Isaiah 55:8-9 (NIV) says,

> "For my thoughts are not your thoughts, neither are your ways my ways," declares the Lord. "As the heavens are higher than the earth, so are my ways higher than your ways and my thoughts than your thoughts."

God's plan didn't look like mine. I would have kept the status quo and tried to hold things together, but God wanted to move us forward and grow us in ways I hadn't imagined.

The Right People at the Right Time

After that painful season, God raised up the right leader to step into the gap that was left. A young lady, who now serves as our campus administrator and pastor, became an invaluable part of our team. Her dedication, passion, and leadership allowed the ministry to continue thriving despite the setback.

She stepped into the role with grace and excellence, and God used her to help sustain and grow the vision even further. What seemed like a devastating loss became an opportunity for God to prove His faithfulness.

Romans8:28 (NIV) reminds us,

> "And we know that in all things God works for the good of those who love him, who have been called according to his purpose."

God turned what the enemy meant for evil into a story of resilience and restoration. He placed the right people in the right places and allowed the vision to continue growing.

Purpose Beyond the Pain

One of the greatest lessons I've learned is that pain can become purpose if we allow God to use it. Instead of letting betrayal paralyze me, I chose to lean into God's guidance and trust that He would redeem the situation.

Sometimes we wonder why God allows painful experiences, but we must remember that God never promised us a pain-free life—He promised to be with us through it all.

Pain may speak loudly, but purpose will always answer if we choose to listen. We must allow the pain to produce purpose rather than paralyze our progress.

Let's make some Application

1. Release the weight

Application: Have you been hurt by someone you trusted? Forgive them, not for their sake, but for yours. Healing starts when you release the weight of bitterness.

2. Trust God's Plan, Even When It Hurts

Jeremiah29:11 says, "For I know the plans I have for you," declares the Lord, "plans to prosper you and not to harm you, plans to give you hope and a future."

Application: Instead of asking, "Why did this happen?" ask, "God, what are You teaching me through this?"

3. Keep Moving Forward

Betrayal almost made me quit. But if I had given up, I would have never seen what God had in store.

Application: What dreams have you buried because of disappointment? It's time to pick them back up.

Bottom Line:

When Pain Speaks, Purpose Answers. Betrayal doesn't define you—how you respond to it does. When people fail you, let God refine you. Your calling is greater than the hurt.

Reflection Questions

Think of a painful moment in your life. How has that pain shaped who you are today?

Have you ever allowed pain to silence your purpose? How can you reclaim your voice and your calling?

Why do you think God allows pain in the lives of those He loves?

How have you seen purpose birthed from your own struggles?

How has someone else's testimony of pain and purpose encouraged you? How can you do the same for others?

What practical steps can you take to turn your pain into purpose today?

Scripture References & Citations

Romans 8:28 - "And we know that in all things God works for the good of those who love Him, who have been called according to His purpose."

Genesis 50:20 - "You intended to harm me, but God intended it for good to accomplish what is now being done, the saving of many lives."

Jeremiah 29:11 - "For I know the plans I have for you," declares the Lord, "plans to prosper you and not to harm you, plans to give you hope and a future."

Chapter 6

The Face of Grace - Embracing God's Work in You

Grace has a face. For many of us, grace is an abstract idea—a theological concept that we hear about in church but struggle to experience in real life. We know God's grace is sufficient, but when life hits us with hardships, disappointments, and unexpected turns, we wonder:

"Is grace really for me?"

I wrestled with that question for years.

When I looked in the mirror and saw scars, I wondered if grace could cover my insecurities.

When I experienced betrayal in ministry, I questioned if grace could heal the wounds people inflicted. When I stepped into unknown territory, unsure of what was ahead, I doubted if grace was strong enough to carry me.

But here's what I discovered—grace is not just an idea, it's an experience. It'sGod's divine hand on your life, carrying you through what should have destroyed you.

- Grace is the reason you survived.

- Grace is the reason you're still standing.

- Grace is the face you see in the mirror—a living testimony of God's faithfulness.

2 Corinthians 12:9 says:

"My grace is sufficient for you, for My power is made perfect in weakness."

Grace is not given when you feel strong—it shows up when you feel weak.

Looking back over my journey, I've realized that God's grace doesn't just rescue—it repositions. Grace took me from hidden to highlighted, from overlooked to overcomer. There were so many moments where I felt unworthy and insignificant, but grace was working behind the scenes to elevate me for God's purpose.

Recognizing Grace in Your Story

Looking back, I can now see grace in places I once overlooked.

I saw grace in my grandmother, who refused to let me skip church when I was younger.

I saw grace in the moments of loneliness, where God's presence became my comfort.

I saw grace in the trials, the setbacks, the heartbreaks—all the moments that could have broken me but instead built me.

Maybe you've been so focused on what's gone wrong in your life that you've missed the evidence of grace.

Sometimes, grace doesn't look like a breakthrough—it looks like survival.

If you're reading this right now, you're a survivor of something.

You've made it through things that should have crushed you. You've endured storms that should have drowned you. And if you're still here, that means God is not done with your story.

The Face of Grace in My Journey

Grace showed up at every major turning point in my life. When I lost my mother, grace sustained me.

When I was misjudged and mistreated, grace strengthened me.

When I was betrayed, grace covered me.

And then, grace showed up again—in a way that humbled me.

When Grace Found Me in Unexpected Places

I wasn't always confident. In fact, there were seasons when I questioned whether I deserved the grace that God had given me.

I wasn't perfect. I didn't always make the best choices. But grace has a way of finding us even when we aren't looking for it.

After planting Relevant Kingdom Center in Exuma, we were making an impact far beyond what I imagined. But deep down, I still wrestled with insecurities.

I often questioned:

"God, do You really see me?"

"Am I really doing enough?"

"Does any of this matter?"

Then, grace did something unexpected.

One day, I received a video message from Pastor David Crank.

At first, I thought, "Surely, this isn't real."

But there it was—a well-known pastor, someone I admired, saying, "Hey, my Bahamas Pastor! I see you, and you're doing an amazing job!"

I was blown away.

Why? Because I thought no one saw us. I thought we were too small, too hidden, too insignificant.

But grace had been working behind the scenes.

Pastor David Crank, who leads Faith Church—a thriving, 18,000-member church with multiple campuses in the U. S.—visited our island not once, but twice. He partnered with RKC in outreach efforts, bringing generosity and support that I never saw coming.

Then grace expanded the reach even further.

Through that connection, I was given the opportunity to speak at Faith Church.

That moment led to even bigger doors opening. I was eventually invited to be featured on The Nicole Crank Show, a nationally broadcasted TV show with international reach across the U. S., Norway, Sweden, Afghanistan, and Europe.

I sat on that set, sharing my testimony on networks like:

Christian Broadcasting Network

Victory Network

NOW TV

TBN Inspire

NBC& ABC (St. Louis & West Palm Beach)

Me. The boy from the Bahamas who once felt overlooked.

The boy who once felt too broken, too scarred, too insignificant.

But grace took me from hidden to highlighted—not for my glory, but for God's.

Psalm 75:6-7 (KJV) says:

> "For promotion cometh neither from the east, nor from the west, nor from the south. But God is the judge: he putts down one, and setts up another."

God saw me when I felt unseen. He called me when I felt unqualified. He promoted me when I felt unworthy.

That's grace.

Revelation 3:8 (NIV) says,

> "See, I have placed before you an open door that no-one can shut."

God was reminding me that when He opens a door, no one can close it—not my doubts, not my insecurities, not my past mistakes.

It wasn't my intention to seek recognition. I was simply being faithful where I was planted. But grace found me, and when God chooses to highlight you, no one can hide you.

God Doesn't Want Us to Hide Our Gifts

One of the biggest lessons I've learned through this journey is that God doesn't want us to hide our gifts. He doesn't want us to diminish our talents or hide our stories just because we feel insecure or unworthy.

Matthew 5:14-16 (NIV) reminds us,

"You are the light of the world. A town built on a hill cannot be hidden. Neither do people light a lamp and put it under a bowl. Instead they put it on its stand, and it gives light to everyone in the house."

God wants our lives to shine for His glory. He wants us to embrace our gifts, our stories, and yes—even our scars. Because the very things we are tempted to hide are the things He uses to draw people to Himself.

There are moments in life when grace doesn't just show up—it chases you down. That's how it felt the day Pastor David Crank called me out on stage. I wasn't prepared for it, didn't see it coming. One minute, I was standing there, hands raised and nodding in affirmation like everything was good. I knew how to wear the face of confidence in front of thousands of people, but inside—I was frozen.

When he pointed to me and said, "God said, EMBRACE THE FACE!" my whole world seemed to stop. My heart pounded so loud I was sure everyone around me could hear it.

Externally, I looked like I was receiving the word—raising my hands, nodding as if I fully believed it. But internally, it felt like a war. Conflicted thoughts hit me like a flood.

Why me? Does he really know what I've been through? Does he see the scars? Does he know the mess behind this moment? A part of me wanted to receive it with boldness, but another part was questioning if I was even worthy of such a declaration. Who was I to be highlighted like that? Who was I to stand in that place when others seemed so much more qualified?

Wrestling with Worth

I couldn't help but feel conflicted. Grace was finding me—again—but I didn't feel worthy of it. There I was, standing in the spotlight, while my mind was replaying every mistake, every scar, every moment of insecurity. I felt like that scarred kid from Nassau, still struggling to see his own reflection as something worth celebrating. I knew God's grace was real, but I couldn't help questioning why He would extend it to someone like me—someone still battling to believe he belonged there.

I wanted to embrace the moment, to let it wash over me like a wave of affirmation, but something in me resisted. *God, are You sure?* I thought. *Do You really see me? Because I don't see what You see. I still see the brokenness, the inadequacy, the fear of being seen and rejected.*

It was as if God was saying, "I see it all—the flaws, the failures, the fears—and I still choose you. You don't have to earn it. You just have to receive it."

But receiving it wasn't easy. When you've spent most of your life feeling less-than, it's hard to believe that grace could actually pursue you, that God could take all the fragments and use them for His glory. I felt undeserving, and honestly, a little exposed. I didn't want people to think I had it all together because the truth was, I didn't.

Learning to Embrace Grace

As Pastor David's words sank in, I realized that grace doesn't wait for you to feel worthy. It meets you in your mess and declares purpose over your pain. I stood there in awe—caught between disbelief and gratitude. I wasn't supposed to be here, in this moment, hearing those words. By all accounts, I should have been disqualified long ago. But God didn't count me out.

It was like He was whispering, "You don't have to be perfect to be purposeful. You don't have to be flawless to be favored." In that moment, I chose to believe it. I chose to accept that God was writing a story bigger than my scars and deeper than my doubts.

Grace doesn't make sense. It doesn't fit neatly into the boxes of human logic. It finds you when you're hiding and calls you when you're hurting. It elevates you when you feel insignificant and says, "You're mine."

A New Perspective

That moment on stage wasn't just a word from a pastor—it was a divine confrontation. Grace was calling out the conflict within me: the desire to be bold and the fear of being exposed. The desire to lead and the fear of being unworthy. It was as if God was saying, "You can't keep hiding behind your own expectations. You don't have to be perfect to be purposeful."

For so long, I had carried a quiet tension between being a pastor and still feeling like that insecure boy from Nassau. It's easy to tell others about God's grace, but it's another thing entirely to receive it for yourself. I had preached freedom while secretly wrestling with my own chains—chains made up of doubt, insecurity, and fear of being truly seen.

For days after that service, I kept replaying the moment in my mind. I couldn't escape the reality that God saw something in me that I didn't see in myself. It forced me to confront the gap between who I was and who God was calling me to be.

I had to make a decision: would I keep living like I had to earn grace, or would I finally embrace it? Would I keep hiding behind a mask of competence, or would I be honest about the areas where I still felt vulnerable and afraid? That word didn't just challenge me—it changed me. It pushed me to drop the facade and walk fully in the freedom that God had given me.

I learned that day that grace doesn't choose you because you're worthy; it chooses you because God is worthy. I didn't have to pretend to have it all together—I just had to be willing to let God use me, scars and all. Grace doesn't just find you when you're strong; it finds you when you're weak and lifts you to where God wants you to be.

That moment on stage didn't just change how I saw myself—it changed how I viewed my calling. I realized that every scar, every moment of insecurity, every time I wanted to give up—God was using it all to shape me into the man He called me to be. Grace wasn't just a concept anymore—it became a reality. I didn't just preach about it; I started living it.

Grace Opens Doors, Not Just for Us but for Others

Every open door God has given me has blessed not just me but those connected to me. It's been a platform to encourage, challenge, and inspire others to step out of the shadows and embrace their calling.

When I think about how God took me from feeling insignificant to being highlighted on global stages, it humbles me. It reminds me that grace is not about me—it's about Him. God doesn't open doors because of our merit but because of His mercy.

So many of us feel like we have to be perfect to be used by God. We think we need to clean up and have it all together before we step into purpose. But the reality is that God uses flawed, imperfect people to showcase His perfect grace.

Justas grace opened doors for me, God wants to open doors for you. Don't let insecurities hold you back. Stop allowing past mistakes to paralyze your progress. When God places an open door in front of you, walk through it with confidence.

- His grace is sufficient.

- His favor is unstoppable.

- His calling is undeniable.

How to Embrace the Face of Grace in Your life?

Many of us struggle to embrace God's grace because we don't feel worthy of it. We look at our past, our mistakes, our shortcomings, and assume grace is for someone else.

But grace is for the unworthy.

- Grace is for the flawed, the broken, the insecure.

- Grace is for the one who feels like they've messed up too many times.

- Grace is for you.

Here's how you can start embracing God's grace today:

1. Stop trying to earn what's already yours

Grace is not a reward for good behavior. It's a gift from God.

Application: Stop striving to be "good enough" for God. Accept that He already calls you enough.

2. Recognize that Grace is working even when you can't see it

Just because you don't feel grace doesn't mean it's not there. God is working behind the scenes.

Application: Take a moment to reflect—where has grace sustained you? Write it down and remind yourself: "God was there, even when I didn't realize it."

3. Let your scars be a testimony of grace

The scars on my face once made me feel ashamed. But now, they are proof that I survived.

Application: What "scars" (physical ,emotional, or spiritual) have you been ashamed of? Instead of hiding them, share your story. Someone else needs the testimony of your survival.

Bottom Line: Grace is Your Reflection

Grace isn't reserved for the perfect—it's designed for the broken. When God calls you, He already knows your flaws. Let His grace be the foundation of your confidence and the strength behind your story

Reflection Questions

When was the last time you truly embraced God's grace rather than trying to earn it?

How has grace carried you through a season when you felt unworthy or insignificant?

What are some "unexpected places" where grace found you? How did it change your perspective?

How can you extend that same grace to yourself and others?

What area of your life still needs to be surrendered to grace? How can you make that choice today?

Scripture References & Citations

2Corinthians 12:9 - "My grace is sufficient for you, for My power is made perfect in weakness."

Luke16:10 - "Whoever can be trusted with very little can also be trusted with much."

Jeremiah 29:11 - "For I know the plans I have for you," declares the Lord, "plans to prosper you

and not to harm you, plans to give you hope and a future."

Psalm 75:6-7 (KJV) - "For promotion cometh neither from the east, nor from the west, nor from the south. But God is the judge: he putts down one, and setts up another."

Revelation 3:8 (NIV) - "See, I have placed before you an open door that no one can shut."

Matthew 5:14-16 (NIV) - "You are the light of the world. A town built on a hill cannot be hidden…"

Chapter 7
Battle-Tested, Purpose-Approved

Leadership isn't glamorous—it's gritty, challenging, and at times, downright exhausting. Leadership can feel like a battlefield. I never imagined that stepping into my calling would mean facing betrayal, opposition, and moments of feeling completely inadequate. Yet, those experiences shaped me in ways I never expected. They weren't just obstacles—they were opportunities for growth, even when it didn't feel like it at the time.

I remember sitting in my office late at night, questioning everything. God, is this really what You called me to? Did I hear You wrong? Am I even capable of leading these people when I can barely keep myself together? The weight of responsibility felt unbearable, and the constant pressure to be strong took its toll on my soul.

Every time betrayal hit, or plans fell apart, I couldn't help but feel like a failure. I thought leadership meant having all the answers, staying composed, and never letting people see the cracks in your armor. But life doesn't work like that—and neither does leadership.

Overtime, I realized that the challenges weren't sent to break me—they were meant to build me. I thought being a strong leader meant being invincible, but God showed me that true strength is found in vulnerability. Leadership wasn't about perfection—it was about persistence. It wasn't about being unbreakable—it was about being unshakable in my faith.

Some people believe that when you step into your calling, everything falls into place. That if God has called you, the road should be smooth. But purpose doesn't come without a price.

Before God positions you, He prepares you.

Before He elevates you, He tests you.

Before He approves you, He allows you to be battle-tested.

James 1:2-4 reminds us:

"Consider it pure joy, my brothers and sisters, whenever you face trials of many kinds, because you know that the testing of your faith produces perseverance. Let perseverance finish its work so that you may be mature and complete, not lacking anything."

God doesn't test you to see if you'll break—He tests you to strengthen what won't.

The Battle of Betrayal: When ThoseClosest to You Turn

Ministry is built on people—but people can also be the source of some of the deepest pain.

One of the hardest seasons of my life came when someone I trusted and mentored betrayed me. He wasn't just a team member—he was family in faith. I had poured into him, believed in him, given him opportunities to lead, and even entrusted him to carry on the vision.

But then, the betrayal came.

The mismanagement of finances.

The deceit behind closed doors.

The loss of trust from the people I was called to shepherd.

I was devastated. I questioned everything.

"God, how could You allow this? I trusted him. I thought he was ready. I put my reputation on the line to believe in him."

But then, God reminded me:

"This battle is not about them—it's about what I'm building in you."

Even Jesus was betrayed—by someone who walked with Him, ate with Him, and witnessed His miracles firsthand.

Luke 22:48 says, "But Jesus asked him, 'Judas, are you betraying the Son of Man with a kiss?'"

Jesus didn't let betrayal stop Him from fulfilling His mission.

Neither can we.

That season tested my ability to forgive, to rebuild trust, and to lead with wisdom.It showed me that the anointing doesn't exempt you from attacks—it prepares you for them.

The Weight of the Call: When the Fire Finds You

From the moment I stepped into ministry, I knew there would be challenges, but I had no idea how deep the fire would go.

I thought the hardest battles I'd face would be external attacks, but some of the deepest wounds came from within—from people I trusted, from leadership I honored, from places I thought were safe.

I thought faithfulness meant I'd always be celebrated, but instead, I learned that being called also means being criticized.

I thought hard work meant quick results, but I learned that growth takes time, obedience, and the ability to endure under pressure.

Sometimes, we believe the pressure we experience is against us, but in reality, it's working for us.

Why Pressure is Necessary

As an aircraft climbs to cruising altitude—about 36,000 feet or higher—the outside air pressure drops dramatically and the air becomes much thinner. Without proper pressurization, the cabin air would also be at low pressure, making it difficult to breathe and even causing severe physiological issues.

Pressurization is not an attack—it's a necessity for survival at high altitudes.

Just like a plane must be pressurized to function at higher altitudes, we must be prepared to handle the pressure of the places God is taking us. Sometimes, the greater the elevation, the greater the pressure required to sustain it.

But that's not the only place where pressure serves a purpose.

The Power of Imperfections: Golf Ball Dimples & Destiny

Ever noticed that a golf ball isn't smooth? It has dimples, dents, and imperfections that may seem like flaws, but in reality, they serve a greater purpose.

Golf balls are designed with dimples to reduce drag and increase lift. These small dents help the ball travel farther and straighter by creating a turbulent boundary layer around the ball.

This reduces air resistance and allows the ball to fly with greater precision and power.

If golf balls were smooth, they wouldn't go as far.

Just like that, sometimes the things we believe are our greatest flaws—the scars, the struggles, the setbacks—are actually the things that propel us further.

What if the very thing you thought was your pain was actually your platform for purpose?

Romans8:28 reminds us:

"And we know that in all things God works for the good of those who love Him, who have been called according to His purpose."

Your pain is not pointless—it's positioning you for something greater.

Battle-Tested: What Every Warrior MustKnow

If you're in a battle right now, you may be wondering:

"God, why is this happening?"

"When will the struggle end?"

"Am I really called for this?"

Here's what I've learned:

1. God's preparation always includes pressure. The greater the calling, the greater the crushing.

2. Not every battle is meant to break you—some are meant to reveal you. God will use storms to show you what you're really made of.

3. If the battle is this hard, the blessing must be even greater. If the enemy is fighting you this hard, it's because he knows what's on the other side of your obedience.

How to Overcome When You'reBattle-Tested

1. Stay Rooted in Prayer

You can't fight battles in your own strength. You need the presence of God to sustain you.

Application: If you're facing a hard season, set aside intentional time in prayer. Even when you don't have words, just sit in His presence.

2. Let the Pain Teach You, Not Break You

Every battle carries a lesson. The goal is not just to survive—but to come out wiser, stronger, and better equipped for the next season.

Application: Journal about what this battle is teaching you. What has God revealed about Himself through this?

3. Remember That Approval Comes After the Testing

Before David became king, he faced lions, bears, and giants. Before Jesus stepped into ministry, He was tested in the wilderness.

1. **Application:** If you're in a battle, it's because your next level is near. Hold on. Keep fighting. Your purpose is being approved.

Bottom Line: Battle-Tested, Purpose-Approved

Grace doesn't make leadership easy—it makes it possible. When your own strength fails, God's grace steps in to carry you through. Stay battle-tested and purpose-approved by leaning on His strength, not your own.

Reflection Questions

What battle are you currently facing that makes you question your purpose and How can you see it differently through God's eyes?

Have past battles made you stronger or more fearful? Why?

What would change in your life if you truly believed that every battle is refining you for your purpose?

Think of a time when you felt unworthy or broken. How did God use that season to strengthen you?

How can you encourage someone else who is going through a battle right now?

Citations & Scripture References

James 1:2-4 - "Consider it pure joy, my brothers and sisters, whenever you face trials of many kinds, because you know that the testing of your faith produces perseverance. Let perseverance finish its work so that you may be mature and complete, not lacking anything."

Romans 8:28 - "And we know that in all things God works for the good of those who loveHim, who have been called according to His purpose."

Luke 22:48 - "But Jesus asked him, 'Judas, are you betraying the Son of Man with a kiss?'"

Psalm 75:6-7 (KJV) - "For promotion cometh neither from the east, nor from the west, nor from the south. But God is the judge: he putts down one, and setts up another."

OutsideSources Referenced

Aircraft Pressurization Concept: Information on cabin pressurization and its necessity for survival at high altitudes is based on general aviation knowledge as found in sources such as the Federal Aviation Administration (FAA) guidelines and aviation safety studies.

Golf Ball Dimples & Aerodynamics: The concept of dimples improving golf ball aerodynamics is widely supported by physics and engineering studies on aerodynamics, as discussed by the United States Golf Association (USGA) and sports science experts.

Chapter 8

The Labels They Gave vs. The Name God Called

L abels can limit, but God's calling liberates.

From the moment we enter this world, people try to define us. Some labels are given in love, others in ignorance, and some in moments of cruelty.

I know what it's like to be mislabeled.

Doctors labeled me with a diagnosis—one that said I wouldn't live past 18.

People labeled me by my appearance—assuming my scars were a sign of weakness rather than survival.

Some labeled me by my background—thinking where I came from would determine how far I could go.

But people's labels don't determine God's plans.

Isaiah 43:1 declares:

"Fear not, for I have redeemed you; I have called you by name; you are mine."

God doesn't consult opinions before He calls you. He doesn't define you by your past. He sees the purpose within you—even when others overlook you.

The Weight of Being Labeled

Sometimes, the heaviest labels aren't the ones others give us—they're the ones we give ourselves.

I have always believed in God's calling over my life, but there were moments when I questioned if I truly belonged.

One of those moments came when I became a part of the House Hold of Faith, a pastors fellowship led by Pastors Nicole and David Crank. This wasn't just any group—it was a by-invitation-only fellowship of highly accomplished pastors. Some of them led churches with congregations the size of an entire island.

And yet, somehow, I was invited to be among them.

While no one in that group ever made me feel like I didn't belong, I began to label myself.

One time, at a gathering they call the "Round Table", where all the pastors in the fellowship meet, I found myself riding on a bus next to Pastor Nicole Crank.

I looked at her and said, "Wow, I can't believe you would have me be a part of this when I'm not as accomplished as most of the pastors here!"

She turned to me with righteous indignation and said:

"Don't ever disqualify yourself by comparing yourself. Context matters, and while you may be on a small island, you guys are making a BIG impact! CONTEXT MATTERS!"

Her words stuck with me.

In reality, I wasn't being limited by others—I was limiting myself.

I had labeled myself small, even though God had called me significant.

So many times, we disqualify ourselves from opportunities because we compare our journey to someone else's.

But God never called us to compete—He called us to complete the work He gave us.

Breaking Free from Self-Imposed Labels

Have you ever counted yourself out before God even finished writing your story?

God never called you "not enough"—that was your own voice.

God never said you didn't belong—that was your insecurity.

God never labeled you by your limitations—He called you according to your purpose.

The truth is, self-imposed labels can be just as dangerous as external ones.

God never asked you to be the best compared to others. He simply asked you to be obedient in your lane.

Maybe you've been labeled by people. Maybe you've carried words spoken over you years ago.

But you don't have to live under those labels anymore.

How you can apply these lessons to your life?

1. Stop Accepting What God Never Assigned

If God didn't say it, it's not yours to carry.

Application: Write down every negative label you've believed about yourself and then cross it out with the truth of what God says about you.

2. Recognize That People's Words Don't Define Your Worth

If people's opinions could determine your destiny, they would have power over God. But God's word trumps every false label.

Application: Speak life-giving affirmations over yourself daily—declare God's truth, not people's lies.

3. Walk in the Name God Gave You

God never called you by your pain, your failures, or your flaws—He called you by His purpose.

Application: Ask God today: "What do You call me? How do You see me?" Then walk boldly in that identity.

Bottom Line: Don't Let Labels Limit You

You are not your comparison. You are not your insecurity. You are not the small version of yourself that fear created.

You are chosen. You are called. You are right where God needs you to be. And no label—from yourself or anyone else—can change that

Reflection Questions

What labels have you carried that didn't come from God? How have they affected your confidence?

How can you break free from the labels given by others and embrace the name God calls you?

Have you ever unintentionally labeled someone else? How can you extend grace and encouragement instead?

What scripture can you declare over your life to remind you of your true identity?

How can you support someone who is struggling with labels that have been placed on them?

Scripture References & Citations

Isaiah 43:1 - "Fear not, for I have redeemed you; I have called you by name; you are mine."

John 15:16 - "You did not choose me, but I chose you and appointed you so that you might go and bear fruit—fruit that will last."

Psalm 139:14 - "I praise You because I am fearfully and wonderfully made; Your works are wonderful, I know that full well."

2Corinthians 12:9 - "My grace is sufficient for you, for my power is made perfect in weakness."

Chapter 9
Made for More

You have no idea how much more there is in you! Life will try to convince you that you've reached your limit—that what you see is all there is. But the truth is, God has planted more in you than you realize. And no matter what you've faced, your story isn't over.

Luke 13:7 (ESV) says:

> "And he said to the vinedresser, 'Look, for three years now I have come seeking fruit on this fig tree, and I find none. Cut it down. Why should it use up the ground?'"

At some point in life, we all face the question of fruitfulness.

Are we growing or staying stagnant?

Are we progressing or making excuses?

God designed you for growth, impact, and more than what you've settled for.

Testify: The Reminder That My Story Wasn't Over

There was a moment when I thought it was over for me. While out of town speaking at an event, I suddenly found myself in a medical emergency. I went to a local urgent care, and before I knew it, they were calling an ambulance. I was rushed to a hospital, where they discovered I had adrenal hemorrhaging—and my kidneys were failing. Doctors quickly assumed that my condition was due to Lupus progression.

- They saw the lesions on my face and scalp and thought, "It has spread from the skin to the internal organs."

- They took over 14 vials of blood, looking for Lupus markers.

- They prepared for a biopsy, assuming my kidneys were permanently damaged.

- My GFR (kidney function) was dangerously low—on the verge of dialysis.

But God...

After the prayers of my pastors, intercessors, and a radical shift in my health, I began to recover.

Today, my GFR is much higher, and I am doing much better. Doctors still can't explain it because they found no traces of Lupus anywhere in my body.

And God reminded me:

"The same God who promised at 12 years old that I would live and not die… is the same God reminding me today that IT'S NOT OVER until He says it's over!"

There is still more for me to do.

There is still kingdom impact to make.

And as long as I remain faithful—God will make me fruitful.

Mr. Miracle Man

My whole life has proven that God is a miracle-working God. And I believe that as you read this book and reflect on your own story, you will see that in every area of your life, God's hand was at work even when you didn't know it.

There were countless times when God was weaving His grace into my story—even when I couldn't see it. One moment that still blows my mind is when I went to a follow-up appointment after that health scare. My doctor, who was not a believer, had previously insisted that I needed to go on dialysis. He was adamant.

But my wife and I refused to accept that prognosis. We held on to the promises of God with fervent faith and unwavering belief. To some, it might have looked like foolish faith, but I knew that I had to trust God with this one. Even when the doctors thought

I was crazy, I couldn't shake the conviction that God was going to heal me.

A few weeks later, I ended up back in the hospital with potassium levels nearly at 8.5—a level considered dangerously high. My kidney function had declined even further, and the doctors were convinced I needed dialysis immediately.

But after we prayed, believed, and hung on to God's promises, my GFR levels returned to normal. I went back to the doctor for a follow-up appointment, and as he walked into the room, he looked at me and said:

"Hey, Mr. Miracle Man!"

Think about that—a doctor who was not a believer, who had previously insisted on dialysis, now greeting me as Mr. Miracle Man. That's just what God does—He makes your life a testament of His miraculous power.

The whole time, God was weaving His purpose through my pain. He was turning what seemed impossible into a testimony. He took what should have ended me and made it a platform for His power.

You Were Designed for Growth

God created you to grow, to develop, and to move forward. When you feel stuck in the same place, stagnant in your calling, or frustrated with your progress ,it's because you weren't made to stay where you are.

• That's why jobs with no opportunity for growth drain you.

• That's why relationships that only take and never give deplete you.

That's why living in a cycle of mediocrity makes you feel unfulfilled.

Genesis1:28 says:

> "Be fruitful and multiply; fill the earth and subdue it."

God didn't just call you to exist—He called you to expand. There is more in you—

• Books the world needs to read.

• Businesses that will bless the kingdom.

• Ideas that will impact generations.

But here's the truth: The root of your frustration might be the lack of fruit in your life.

Stay Connected to the Source

The only way to step into the "more" God has for you is to stay connected to Him.

John 15:5 (ESV) says:

> "I am the vine; you are the branches. Whoever abides in me and I in him, he it is that bears much fruit, for apart from me you can do nothing."

If you want open doors in this next season, you can't just be near God—

He has to be dwelling within you.

STAY IN HIM!

• Don't walk away from God because people in the church disappointed you.

• Don't dismiss His calling because it didn't happen when or how you expected.

• Don't settle for an "almost Christian" life and expect to reap the full blessings of obedience.

My prayer is simple:

"God, I don't want a lukewarm life—I want a fruitful life!"

The Truth Is in the Fruit

Jesus tells a parable about a fig tree in Luke 13:6-8:

> "A man had a fig tree planted in his vineyard, and he came seeking fruit on it and found none."

That fig tree was taking up space but not producing.

I often ask myself:

"When God looks at my life, does He see fruit? Or does He see wasted potential?"

The man in the parable says, "Cut it down. It's using up the ground."

In other words, unproductive attachments drain life from what God is trying to grow in you.

Surround Yourself with People Who Elevate You

I'm grateful for Pastors David and Nicole Crank. Since they came into my life, I've experienced:

- A stronger marriage.

- A healthier ministry.

- Better finances.

- More confidence in my calling.

Because here's the truth: WHO and WHAT you surround yourself with matters.

Some people elevate you—some people limit you.

Some places push you to grow—some places keep you stagnant.

If you want to walk in the "more" God has for you, you have to be willing to step into environments that stretch you.

The Power of Grace

Luke 13:8-9 shows us a powerful moment of grace.

The vinedresser says:

"Sir, let it alone this year also, until I dig around it and put on manure. Then if it should bear fruit next year, well and good; but if not, you can cut it down."

God isn't cutting you down—He's cultivating you!

• Sometimes, He allows disruption to push you into growth.

• Sometimes, He allows "manure" (stinky situations) to fertilize the soil of your future.

• Sometimes, He removes people not to punish you, but to prepare you.

John 15:2 reminds us:

"Every branch in Me that does not bear fruit, He takes away; and every branch that does bear fruit, He prunes, so that it will bear more fruit."

Pruning isn't punishment—it's preparation. If God is cutting something out of your life, it's because He's making room for more.

Bottom Line:

There's More in You

Your story isn't over.

God's not done with you.

You were made for more.

- More growth.

- More impact.

- More fruitfulness.

And as long as you stay faithful—God will make you fruitful.

Application: How to Step into Your More

1. Stop Settling for Stagnancy

Growth requires movement. Don't get stuck in a comfort zone.

Application: Identify one area in your life where you've settled and make a plan to take a step forward today.

2. Recognize God's Hand in Your Story

Even when you can't see it, God is weaving His purpose through your pain.

Application: Reflect on a time when you thought it was over, but God turned it around. Write it down and declare:

"God is not done with me yet!"

3. Surround Yourself with Visionaries

The people around you should push you to grow and pursue God's best.

Application: Identify someone who inspires you and reach out to them for encouragement or mentorship.

Reflection Questions

1. In what areas of your life have you settled for less than God's best?

2. What would it look like to believe that you were truly made for more?

3. What practical step can you take today to move toward the "more" that God has for you?

4. Who in your life challenges you to think bigger and pursue your potential? How can you thank them?

5. How can you begin walking boldly into the more that God has prepared for you?

Scripture References & Citations

Luke 13:7 - "Look, for three years now I have come seeking fruit on this fig tree, and I find none. Cut it down. Why should it use up the ground?"

John 15:2 - "Every branch in Me that does not bear fruit, He takes away; and every branch that does bear fruit, He prunes, so that it will bear more fruit."

Genesis 1:28 - "Be fruitful and multiply; fill the earth and subdue it."

John 15:5 - "I am the vine; you are the branches... apart from me you can do nothing."

Chapter 10

Embrace the Face - Owning Your Story Without Fear

What if the thing you're hiding is the thing God wants to heal? For years, I believed that if I was just good enough, accomplished enough, and spiritually disciplined enough, I wouldn't have to deal with the parts of me I wanted to keep hidden.

I learned how to mask my struggles with performance.

I learned how to hide my imperfections behind success.

I learned how to cover my insecurities with outward strength.

But God wasn't impressed with what I was trying to project. He wanted the real me. He wanted the man behind the armor.

The Naaman Complex: Hiding Behind the Armor

One of the most powerful stories in Scripture that speaks to hiding behind status, accomplishments, and appearance is found in 2 Kings 5:1-14—the story of Naaman.

Naaman was a respected and successful commander. He was a man of valor, strength, and honor.

But beneath all his victories, medals, and prestige—he had a problem.

A problem he tried to hide. Leprosy. Naaman wore his armor well. He stood before men as a warrior. But when the armor came off, he was diseased.

- He was celebrated publicly but suffering privately.

- He was strong on the outside but decaying on the inside.

- He had influence but still felt inadequate.

AndI know that feeling well.

The Weight of Hiding

For years, I felt like I had to be perfect.

- Perfect in my commitment to God.

- Perfect in my character.

- Perfect in my public perception.

I didn't want anyone to see my weaknesses, struggles, or insecurities. But hiding doesn't heal you—it hurts you.

Like Naaman, I had leprosy in my soul.

- I wasn't struggling with a skin disease, but I was struggling internally.

- I wasn't covered in sores, but I was covered in shame.

One of the hardest things I ever had to do was acknowledge that I wasn't as strong as I pretended to be. And one of the most freeing things I ever experienced was realizing that God wasn't asking for my perfection—He was asking for my surrender.

The Moment of Exposure and Grace

There was a time in Bible college when I was wrestling with a hidden battle. I was in a place where I was learning the Word, growing in faith, and preparing for ministry, but at the same time, I was battling something in secret.

Pornography.

I felt disqualified because of it.

I felt like if people knew, they wouldn't respect me.

I felt like God was disappointed in me.

And one night, after a Wednesday service, I couldn't hold it in anymore.

Sitting on a bench near "the monument" by our dorms on a beautiful fall night, I looked at Sharai— The woman who would later become my wife—And I told her the truth.

I told her about my struggle.

I told her about the guilt I carried.

It old her about how unworthy I felt.

I braced for judgment. But instead, I received grace.

She looked at me—not with condemnation, but with love.

She prayed for me—not to embarrass me, but to cover me.

She reminded me—not of my failure, but of God's ability to restore.

And then, she began to sing...

"How many times do I go against Your will, then You forgive me... But yet I still turn around and do the things, the things I shouldn't do..."

The lyrics of "Calling My Name" by Hezekiah Walker filled the air, and something inside of me broke. I sat there, overwhelmed. Tears fell. My heart opened. At that moment, I wasn't just hearing a song—I was hearing God's voice.

He wasn't calling me out—He was calling me back.

God wasn't asking me to perform for Him—

He was asking me to be real with Him.

Dipping in the River of Grace

Naaman's healing didn't come until he humbled himself. At first, he resisted. When the prophet Elisha told him to go dip in the Jordan River seven times, Naaman was offended.

"That river is dirty."

"There has to be another way."

"I'm too important to do that."

But until he was willing to go low, he couldn't be lifted. Until he was willing to take off the armor—he couldn't be healed.

2 Kings 5:14 (ESV) says:

"So he went down and dipped himself seven times in the Jordan, according to the word of the man of God, and his flesh was restored like the flesh of a little child, and he was clean."

For Naaman, his breakthrough required humility.

For me, my healing required accountability.

And for you, your freedom will require honesty.

Stop Hiding. Start Healing.

The enemy wants you to stay hidden.

- He wants you to keep your struggles in the dark.

- He wants you to carry the weight of perfection.

- He wants you to believe that your scars make you unworthy.

But God is saying:

"If you'll take off the armor, I will heal what's underneath."

Psalm 34:18 (NIV) says:

"The Lord is close to the brokenhearted and saves those who are crushed in spirit."

You don't have to hide behind strength.

You don't have to pretend everything is perfect.

You don't have to carry the weight of

trying to hold it all together.

Come as you are.

God can't heal who you pretend to be—

He can only heal who you truly are.

How to Own Your Story Without Fear.

1. Be Honest with Yourself

You can't heal what you won't admit.

Scripture: Psalm 32:5 - "Then I acknowledged my sin to you and did not cover up my iniquity. I said, 'I will confess my transgressions to the Lord.' And you forgave the guilt of my sin."

2. Stop Hiding Behind Your Accomplishments

Success doesn't heal wounds—only surrender does.

Scripture: Jeremiah 17:9 - "The heart is deceitful above all things and beyond cure. Who can understand it?"

3. Surround Yourself with People Who Cover You, Not Condemn You

The right people will push you toward healing, not shame you into silence.

Scripture: Galatians 6:2 - "Carry each other's burdens, and in this way you will fulfill the law of Christ."

Bottom Line: Own Your Story. Walk in Freedom.

- You don't have to wear the armor anymore.

- You don't have to pretend to be perfect.

- You don't have to hide your wounds—God wants to heal them.

It's time to dip in the river of grace. Because the moment you stop hiding is the moment healing begins.

Reflection Questions

1. What parts of your story have you been hesitant to share? Why?

2. How would owning your story change your confidence and influence?

3. Why is it important to embrace the face God gave you, both physically and spiritually?

4. What truth do you need to declare over your life today to walk in freedom?

5. Who could be impacted by your story if you shared it without fear?

Scripture References & Citations

2 Kings 5:1-14 - The story of Naaman's healing after removing his armor and dipping in the Jordan.

Psalm 34:18 - "The Lord is close to the brokenhearted and saves those who are crushed in spirit."

Psalm 32:5 - "Then I acknowledged my sin to you and did not cover up my iniquity."

Jeremiah 17:9 - "The heart is deceitful above all things and beyond cure."

Galatians 6:2 - "Carry each other's burdens, and in this way you will fulfill the law of Christ."

Chapter 11
Bottom Line - Call to Action

You've read the stories.

You've seen the scars.

You've walked through the pages of my journey.

But now, this isn't just about me.

This is about you.

Every thing you've been through—

Every battle you've fought—

Every label you've had to reject—

Every moment you've questioned your worth—

It was never meant to break you.

It was never meant to define you.

It was meant to prepare you.

Because God doesn't waste pain.

God doesn't call you by your past—He calls you by your purpose.

Your Story Isn't Over

Maybe you've spent years believing the lies—

That your scars make you unworthy.

That your past makes you unusable.

That your struggles make you less than.

But today, I need you to hear this: YOUR STORY ISN'T OVER.

God is still writing.

God is still moving.

God is still calling you higher, deeper, and into more.

Ephesians 2:10 (NIV) says:

> "For we are God's handiwork, created in Christ Jesus to do good works, which God prepared in advance for us to do."

You weren't just made to survive—you were made to make a difference.

You weren't just saved for yourself—you were called to impact others.

The world needs what's inside of you.

What Will You Do with What God Has Given You?

The worst thing you can do after reading this book is go back to life as usual.

- To go back to hiding what God wants to use.

- To go back to playing small when you were made for more.

- To go back to insecurity and fear instead of walking in faith.

Because now you know the truth.

Now you know that—

Your scars don't disqualify you.

Your past doesn't cancel your future.

Your story is a testimony that someone else needs to hear.

So the question isn't, "Can God use me?" The question is, "Will I let Him?"

No More Excuses. It's Time to Move.

- No more waiting for the "perfect" time.

- No more letting fear talk you out of your purpose.

- No more allowing past pain to paralyze your future progress.

Today is the day you say:

I will embrace my scarsI will own my story.

I will step into my purpose.

I will stop waiting and start walking in what God has for me.

Because purpose is not found in perfection—it's found in obedience.

What's Your Next Step?

Everyone's journey looks different, but one thing remains true:

You cannot stay where you are and go where God is calling you.

So what's your next move?

1.Maybe it's time to share your testimony.

Speak your truth—someone needs to hear it.

2.Maybe it's time to launch that vision God placed in you.

Start the business, the book, the ministry—move on what God gave you.

3.Maybe it's time to release the weight of the past.

Forgive who hurt you. Drop the shame. Walk free.

4. Maybe it's time to fully surrender to God's call.

No more halfway faith—go all in.

James 1:22 (NLT) says:

"But don't just listen to God's word. You must do what it says. Otherwise, you are only fooling yourselves."

- This is your moment.
- This is your call to action.
- This is your time to embrace the face, own your story, and walk into purpose—unapologetically.

Bottom Line: You Were Made for This.

- No more running.
- No more doubting.
- No more holding back.

You were made for such a time as this. Your scars are evidence of survival. Your testimony is proof of God's power.

And your story is just getting started.

Now go—live it out.

Reflection Questions

What is the bottom line God has spoken to you through this book?

What step of faith are you willing to take to fully embrace your purpose?

How will you use your story to impact others from this day forward?

What excuses have you allowed to hold you back from walking in purpose?

What will change in your life now that you've read this book?

Scripture References & Citations

Ephesians 2:10 - "For we are God's handiwork, created in Christ Jesus to do good works, which God prepared in advance for us to do."

James 1:22 - "But don't just listen to God's word. You must do what it says."

REFLECTIONS

Reflections & Reminders

As you turn the final page, take a moment to pause, reflect, and personalize what this journey has meant to you. This empty page isn't just for notes—they're for your **revelations, breakthroughs**, and **next steps**. Your story matters. Your scars speak. And your voice is needed. Write here. Dream here. Grow here.

Reflections & Reminders

Acknowledgements

This book is more than just words on a page—it is the result of faith, love, sacrifice, and unwavering support.

First and foremost, I give all glory to God—the One who took my scars and turned them into a testimony, the One who has proven time and time again that His plans are greater than my pain.

To my wife, Sharai—there are not enough words to thank you. You put up with the late nights, the long hours, and the moments when my mind was buried in writing instead of present with you. Your love, patience, and support made this book possible. Thank you for believing in me when I struggled to believe in myself.

To my children, D'Mari, Damir, Shamir, and Dashuan—thank you for allowing me the time and space to focus on completing this work. My greatest prayer is that you will always walk boldly in your identity, knowing that you are called, chosen, and loved by God.

To Pastors David & Nicole Crank—your spiritual investment in my life has meant more than you know. Pastor David, the night you called me out on stage and said, "God said, EMBRACE THE FACE!" was the moment everything shifted for me. It wasn't just a word—it was a catalyst that gave me the confidence to step into my identity, lead with boldness, and write this book. Thank you for seeing what God had already placed inside of me and calling it forth.

To Kevin & Karla Gagnon—your love, support, and unwavering deposit into our lives is something we do not take for granted. You have been there for us in ways that only God could have orchestrated. Thank you for always believing, always pouring in, and always reminding us of the goodness of God's grace.

To everyone who has been a part of this journey—those who prayed, encouraged, supported, and spoke life into me when I needed it most—this book is for you.

And to every reader, every person who has wrestled with identity, shame, and self-doubt—may these pages remind you that God has never called you by your scars, but by your purpose. Now go embrace the face—walk boldly into the life God has called you to live!

With gratitude,

Duerre Thomas

Final Author's Note

To every reader who has journeyed through these pages—

Your story matters.

You may not have the same scars I do, but I know you have a story that is uniquely yours.

Maybe your wounds aren't physical—maybe they're emotional, spiritual, or deeply personal.

Maybe life has left marks on your heart that no one else can see.

Maybe you've walked through seasons of pain, disappointment, and questioning.

But here's what I want you to know:

Your pain is not in vain.

God has a plan for your life, and even when you can't see it—He is working.

Romans 8:28 reminds us:

"And we know that in all things God works for the good of those who love him, who have been called according to his purpose."

Purpose in the Process

One of the hardest truths to accept is that God doesn't always prevent the pain—butHe always has a purpose in it.

• He didn't send the betrayal, but He will use it to refine you.

• He didn't send the loss, but He will use it to deepen your faith.

He didn't send the storm, but He will use it to strengthen your foundation.

Like Job, sometimes God allows tests—not to break us, but to build us.

And my prayer for you is that you pass the test.

Not just that you survive the pain—but that you embrace the journey and walk in your purpose.

Your Next Step

This book isn't just about my scars—it's about your healing, your growth, your story.

The real question now is: What will you do with what God has given you?

• Will you keep hiding, or will you walk in confidence?

• Will you let the past define you, or will you step into your future?

• Will you stay where you are, or will you trust God's plan and move forward?

You are not an accident. You are not forgotten.

You are not a mistake. You were created for a purpose, and God is still writing your story.

Final Words: Embrace the Journey, Walk in Purpose

So here's my challenge to you:

- Embrace the journey—every scar, every lesson, every step.

- Trust that God is ordering your steps, even when you

don't understand.

- Stop waiting for the perfect time to step into your calling—the time is now.
- Walk boldly, knowing that you were never meant to blend in, but to stand out.

If God could take my scars and turn them into a testimony, Then surely, He can take your story and use it for His glory.

Now go—Embrace the Face. Own your story. Walk in purpose.

With gratitude and faith,

Duerre Thomas

Additional Resources

This book is just the beginning. Your journey of embracing your scars, walking in confidence, and stepping into purpose continues.

Here are some next steps and resources to help you apply the lessons from this book to your life:

Reflection & Journal Prompts

Use these questions to deepen your personal growth and transformation:

1. Embracing Your Story

- What are the scars (physical, emotional, or spiritual) that you've struggled to accept?

- How has God used past pain to shape your purpose?

- What is one area of your life where you still need to embrace your identity inChrist?

2. Walking in Confidence

- Where in your life have you been holding back because of fear or insecurity?

- What would change if you fully believed that God has called you for more?

- Write a declaration of who God says you are (using scriptures from this book)and speak it daily.

3. Answering the Call to Purpose

- What has God placed in your heart that you've been hesitant to pursue?

- What practical steps can you take today to start moving toward your God-given assignment?

- Who can you share your story with to encourage them in their journey?

Books by Duerre Thomas

Recommended Reading & Next Steps

Looking to grow even deeper in your faith, leadership, and confidence? Here are some additional resources to help you continue your journey:

TheBible - The ultimate source of truth and transformation.

Books by Duerre Thomas

Leading a Generation:

A powerful resource for leaders who want to impact the next generation with confidence, faith, and purpose.

Get it on Amazon

Moments with God for Teens

A devotional designed to help teenagers strengthen their faith and navigate life with God's wisdom.

Get it on Amazon

• Real Questions, Real Answers: A Guide for Teens

A guide tackling the toughest questions young people face about faith, life, and purpose.

Get it on Amazon

Other Resources

- Devotionals & Small Group Studies - Find faith-based studies that will help you apply biblical truths to your daily walk.

- Mentorship & Coaching Opportunities - If you're looking to go deeper, seek out a mentor or leader who can guide you in this next season.

Ways to Stay Connected

If this book impacted you, I'd love to hear from you!

Here's how you can stay connected:

EMAIL: Madpastor1@gmail.com

Scripture Index

Old Testament Scriptures

Genesis

• Genesis 1:28 - "Be fruitful and multiply; fill the earth and subdue it."

Exodus

• Exodus 14:14 - "The Lord will fight for you; you need only to be still."

Deuteronomy

- Deuteronomy 31:6 - "Be strong and courageous. Do not be afraid or terrified because of them, for the Lord your God goes with you; he will never leave you nor forsake you."

Isaiah

- Isaiah 43:1 - "Fear not, for I have redeemed you; I have called you by name; you are mine."

- Isaiah 53:5 - "But He was wounded for our transgressions, He was bruised for our iniquities; the chastisement for our peace was upon Him, and by His stripes we are healed."

- Isaiah 62:2 - "You will be called by a new name that the mouth of the Lord will bestow."

Jeremiah

- Jeremiah 17:9 - "The heart is deceitful above all things and beyond cure. Whocan understand it?"

- Jeremiah 29:11 - "For I know the plans I have for you," declares the Lord,"plans to prosper you and not to harm you, plans to give you hope and a future."

Psalms

- Psalm 32:5 - "Then I acknowledged my sin to you and did not cover up myiniquity. I said, 'I will confess my transgressions to the Lord.' And youforgave the guilt of my sin."

- Psalm 34:18 - "The Lord is close to the brokenhearted and saves those who arecrushed in spirit."

- Psalm 61:2 - "From the end of the earth I will cry to You, when my heart isoverwhelmed; lead me to the rock that is higher than I."

- Psalm 75:6-7 (KJV) - "For promotion cometh neither from the east, nor from thewest, nor from the south. But God is the judge: he putteth down one, andsetteth up another."

- Psalm 118:17 - "I will not die but live, and will proclaim what the Lord hasdone."

- Psalm 139:14 - "I praise You because I am fearfully and wonderfully made; Your works are wonderful, I know that full well."

New Testament Scriptures

Matthew

- Matthew 5:14-16 - "You are the light of the world. A city set on a hill cannot be hidden... let your light shine before others, that they may see your good deeds and glorify your Father in heaven."

Luke

- Luke 6:7 - "And he said to the vinedresser, 'Look, for three years now I have come seeking fruit on this fig tree, and I find none. Cut it down. Why should it use up the ground?'"

- Luke 13:6-8 - "A man had a fig tree planted in his vineyard, and he came seeking fruit on it and found none."

- Luke 13:8-9 - "Sir, let it alone this year also, until I dig around it and put on manure. Then if it should bear fruit next year, well and good; but if not, you can cut it down."

John

- John 15:2 - "Every branch in Me that does not bear fruit, He takes away; and every branch that does bear fruit, He prunes, so that it will bear more fruit."

- John 15:5 - "I am the vine; you are the branches. Whoever abides in me and I in him, he it is that bears much fruit, for apart from me you can do nothing."

- John 15:16 - "You did not choose me, but I chose you and appointed you so that you might go and bear fruit—fruit that will last."

Acts

- Acts 16:25-26 - "About midnight Paul and Silas were praying and singing hymns to God, and the other prisoners were listening to them. Suddenly there was such a violent earthquake that the foundations of the prison were shaken. At once all the prison doors flew open, and everyone's chains came loose."

Romans

- Romans 8:1 - "There is now no condemnation for those who are in Christ Jesus."

- Romans 8:28 - "And we know that in all things God works for the good of thosewho love Him, who have been called according to His purpose."

- Romans 10:9 - "If you declare with your mouth, 'Jesus is Lord,' and believe in your heart that God raised him from the dead, you will be saved."

1 Corinthians

- 1Corinthians 15:58 - "Therefore, my dear brothers and sisters, stand firm. Let nothing move you. Always give yourselves fully to the work of the Lord, because you know that your labor in the Lord is not in vain."

2 Corinthians

- 2Corinthians 4:8-9 - "We are hard pressed on every side, but not crushed; perplexed, but not in despair; persecuted, but not abandoned; struck down, but not destroyed."

- 2Corinthians 12:9 - "My grace is sufficient for you, for My power is made perfect in weakness."

Galatians

- Galatians 6:2 - "Carry each other's burdens, and in this way you will fulfill the law of Christ."

- Galatians 6:4 - "Pay careful attention to your own work, for then you will get the satisfaction of a job well done, and you won't need to compare yourself to anyone else."

Ephesians

- Ephesians 2:10 - "For we are God's handiwork, created in Christ Jesus to do good works, which God prepared in advance for us to do."

- Ephesians 3:20 - "Now to him who is able to do immeasurably more than all we ask or imagine, according to his power that is at work within us."

James

- James 1:2-4 - "Consider it pure joy, my brothers and sisters, whenever you face trials of many kinds, because you know that the testing of your faith produces perseverance. Let perseverance finish its work so that you may be mature and complete, not lacking anything."

- James 1:22 - "But don't just listen to God's word. You must do what it says.Otherwise, you are only fooling yourselves."

Revelation

- Revelation 12:11 - "They overcame him by the blood of the Lamb and by the word of their testimony."

About the Author

Duerre Thomas is a passionate pastor, author, and speaker whose life is a testimony that God can take pain and turn it into purpose. From an early age, he faced hardship, loss, and rejection—but instead of allowing his scars to define him, he allowed God to refine him.

Starting in ministry at just 21years old, he spent 11 years as a youth pastor in Freeport, Bahamas, where he helped grow one of the largest youth conferences in the nation, impacting thousands of young people. Later, he and his wife, Sharai Thomas, took a bold leap of faith, relocating their family to Exuma, Bahamas, where they plantedRelevant Kingdom Center (RKC) a church built on the heart of reaching the de-churched and unchurched.

His journey was never easy. From experiencing personal loss and struggles with a chronic illness to enduring betrayal in ministry, Duerre has walked through fire and favor. But through it all, God has been faithful. His story of transformation and perseverance has led him to global platforms, where he has shared his testimony on national television, international ministry stages, and leadership conferences.

Beyond ministry, Duerre is a dedicated husband and father. He and Sharai are blessed with four amazing sons—D'Mari, twin boys Damir and Shamir, and their youngest, Dashuan. His greatest desire is that his children live out their faith with even greater boldness and embrace their scars as part of God's plan for their lives.

Duerre now leads two thriving church campuses.

RKC Bahamas and RKC Florida—continuing to impact lives through faith, outreach, and leadership. His journey from feeling hidden to highlighted is a testament that God's grace is greater than any setback.

For more, follow Duerre Thomas at:

INSTAGRAM- @PASTORDUERRETHOMAS

FACEBOOK– @DUERRETHOMAS

www.ingramcontent.com/pod-product-compliance
Lightning Source LLC
Chambersburg PA
CBHW021956090426
42811CB00001B/52